THEORY OF SOCIAL EXCHANGE AND PERSONHOOD

This publication is designed to provide accurate and authoritative information regarding the subject matter covered. While the publisher and author have used their best efforts in preparing this book, they make no representations or warranties with respect to the accuracy or completeness of the contents of this book and specifically disclaim any implied warranties of merchantability or fitness for a particular purpose.

The advice and strategies contained herein may not be suitable for your situation. You should consult with a professional when appropriate. Neither the publisher nor the author shall be liable for any loss of profit or any other commercial damages, including but not limited to special, incidental, consequential, personal, or other damages.

No portion of this book may be reproduced in any form without written permission from the publisher or author, except as permitted by U.S. copyright law.

Established September 2024
New York, NY
United States of America

Cover: Image by edith lüthi

Published by McWest & Associates
ISBN: 978-1-971928-28-9

THEORY OF SOCIAL EXCHANGE AND PERSONHOOD

Baruch Menache

Part I – From Concept to Deed 1

CONVERSATION AND CONCEPT REFINEMENT 1

THE CONCEPTUAL LANDSCAPE AND THE TIMING OF ACTION 8

ACTION, SACRIFICE AND SERVICE 13

BRIDGING CONCEPTUAL AND MATERIAL REALMS 15

Part II – Intimacy, Power, and Persona 17

DIALOGUE AND NARRATIVE 19

MANIPULATION AND RESPONSE 23

MIRROR DYNAMICS IN RELATIONSHIPS 27

GOSSIP AND POWER PLAYS 29

STAGES OF GROUP FORMATION 35

VALUING ATTENTION 41

TRADING EXPOSURE 43

ADOLESCENT CRITIQUE OF SOCIAL EXCHANGE SYSTEMS 46

DUAL DYNAMICS OF EXCHANGE 48

Part III – Dynamics of Potential 51

POTENTIAL: INTERNAL VS. EXTERNAL 53

POTENTIAL PROCESSES (ACTUAL VS. LATENT) 54

POTENTIAL IN CONTEXT (INDIVIDUAL AND COLLECTIVE) 71

SOCIALITY, DETACHMENT, AND STRUCTURAL DRIFT 77

POTENTIAL AND ACTUALITY 85

Part IV – Actualizing Personhood 101

CHILDHOOD ACTUALIZATION 103

PREREQUISITES: BIOLOGICAL ACTUALIZATION 107

ACTUALIZATION: PROCESS AND REPRESENTATION 111

FRAGMENTATION OF THE PSYCHE 119

Part V – Capabilities of the Collective 121

THE COMMUNAL CHARACTER 123

FIRST: FREEDOM FROM PERSONAL EXISTENCE 123

SECOND: PROCESSING COLLECTIVE INFORMATION 124

THIRD: IMPARTIAL REPRESENTATION 124

FOURTH: THE PERPETUAL STATE OF HAPPINESS 126

FIFTH: THE ILLUSION OF PERFECTION 128

SIXTH: THE FATE OF THE COMMUNAL BODY 133

SUSTAINING THE COMMUNAL CHARACTER 135

FIRST: INTEGRATION WITHIN SOCIAL CONSCIOUSNESS 135

SECOND: WILLINGNESS TO INTERACT 136

THIRD: INTERNAL UNITY 136

CONTAGIOUS IDENTITY 141

MAINTAINING THE COMMUNAL BODY 153

INTEGRATION, DOUBT, AND UNIFICATION 157

INDIVIDUALITY AND THE COMMUNAL BODY 158

INTIMACY, INDIVIDUALITY, AND THE COMMUNAL BODY 164

PUBLIC SPEECH AND MATERIALITY 171

REEXAMINING CLASS SYSTEMS 177

ential

Part VI – The Social Life of Speech 185

INFLECTION AND RELATIONSHIPS 187

UPSPEAK AND SOCIAL DYNAMICS 191

PSYCHOLOGICAL PURPOSE: EMOTIONAL RISK MANAGEMENT 193

EMOTION OF PROTECTION VS. ANCHORING AWAY FROM INDIVIDUALITY 195

PERFORMING EMOTION 196

TRAGEDY VS. COMEDY 197

CONTRIVED INTIMACY OF A SITCOM 199

RELATABILITY AND SOCIAL INTEGRATION 201

RELATABILITY AND RECIPROCITY OF DESIGN 203

DUALITY OF RELATABILITY 209

Part I – From Concept to Deed

CONVERSATION AND CONCEPT REFINEMENT

THE TRANSITION from conversation to action is a worthwhile inquiry, for the objective of conversation is to negotiate an understanding of the conceptual landscape so that the realm of action need not be a long or deliberate ordeal. The manifestation of activity will usually be the ultimate reason for conceptual dealings, akin to the propagation of the species according to the evolutionary principle.[1]

Action is inevitable, but it is most effective when preceded by a thorough resolution within the conceptual framework. Once such resolution is achieved, the necessary activity proceeds naturally and without friction.

To frame this transition from concept to action in familiar narrative terms, we may turn to the archetype of the hero's journey—a structure where an individual encounters trials not merely as obstacles, but as catalysts for a deeper conceptual evolution. The hero's journey exemplifies the trial-and-error process—a preliminary experience where they conceptually face adversarial positions—notwithstanding activity without the existential aspect—and this will be done so that the inevitable action to later arise will be a simple manifestation of the conceptual foreground.

---

[1] Charles Darwin, *The Descent of Man.*

Another point to consider is that the final accomplishment does not serve as a platform for further directives. Rather, the action was a sequential necessity—not a substance in itself, but a product of conceptual preparation.

The conceptual realm will not follow the material for a further interplay of successful activity, and the hero will be for others what they cannot be for themselves. This becomes an inspiration for the hero to enter into the domain of self-sacrifice, as they find an empty psyche on the other side of their activity, wishing to conclude at the peak of the hero's action.

Action will be much like the performance of opening a door that contains neither conceptual nor material energy. It is a matter of fact—something most would not consider a necessary expense of life. There is no contest to its reality, and it will flow efficiently toward its proper course without setbacks, human interest, or concern. The adversarial components that prey on vulnerability will find such earnest conceptual foreplay in which the exposed vulnerabilities are ignored. The conceptual or material leverage utilized for the threatening exposition of vulnerabilities—although quite an exchange—is of little interest to the already built conceptual structure, which cannot be undone by vulnerability.

Similar to a structure, its establishment is vulnerable and can be swayed easily in altered directions, while in the later stages the most intricate vulnerability appears insignificant to the already developed circumstance. The first point of interaction at the very beginning of the structure—a single human thought—is most susceptible to vulnerability, as it can be dismissed with another thought.

These material actions are not considered an expenditure, even by those ruminating in expanded conceptual landscapes, because there is no available data that would concern that realm. When we expand the concept of doorways and their associated realms, we begin to introduce competing elements and details that could transform even the simple act of opening a door into a matter of negotiation and sacrifice. To illustrate this in everyday terms, walking down the street may seem like a straightforward act, but for someone who understands its conceptual nuances, it becomes an ongoing process of negotiation.

This is why the advent of communal modes of transportation has been a great service to the conceptual realm: it does not require any material activity for a journey. It becomes a non-activity, which does not require an expense to the conceptual realm. The only cost is the transition toward it, away from it, and the time it occupies. However, this will not remove the cost of movement in which the destination changes, however it may occur. The conceptual realm seeks retribution because there is a cost that requires a balance for its metabolic investment.

Social action, unlike mundane tasks such as opening a door, inherently involves conceptual negotiation because it reflects broader existential considerations and human intentionality. The highlight of action exists specifically in contrast to the conceptual realm, in which it is both adjacent and conflicting. Were it an action not residing within the realm of conceptuality, it would be lost as a term of action and instead would be a natural reality—undeserving of and untouched by definition.

The term *activity* is isolated to that which is adjacent to the conceptual realm. However, conversation is a method that lays out the conceptual realm so that it can be transacted in a manner suitable for fusion between participating parties. Each participant answers to the conceptual fissure or mishandling of the other, so that with one extreme noted, the other may counteract with its opposite to fulfill a refined conceptual landscape.

The objective of the participant proposing input is to ingest the conceptual information as their own. If no counterargument is presented, this becomes an understanding for both parties. If the fissure is not addressed, both participants will leave the conversation with unresolved gaps, rendering the dialogue counterproductive to conceptual growth.

Conceptual refinement in a conversation is the ability to adapt to a more advanced conceptual backdrop. Much like the fissure observed by one party, there is a ubiquitous fissure at the edge of the conceptual realm—a desire for further advancement. When we study this realm, we find that any promise of advancement essentially reflects the recognition of a fissure that must be filled.

A clear example can be seen in cognitive development: the conceptual realm of a child may begin with general categories; however, upon maturity, there is an advancement toward more specific particulars, which will remove much of that generality. The fissure has repeatedly been nearby since they generalized systems without taking notice of their intrinsic particulars, and maturity brings about the substantiation of those fissures. The general categories will still be a part of that conceptual realm, although they will not be the entirety of the mature landscape. As demonstrated in Plato's *Meno*, Socrates argues that mathematical insight is not newly acquired but rather remembered from the soul's prior knowledge (Meno, 81d–85d).[2]

Thus, conversation becomes the means by which fissures—whether evident in extreme positions or subtle in the case of a demand for advancement—are addressed. Technically, with two proponents who continue indefinitely in proper conversation, there should be continuous advancements for the conceptual realm. The reason that conversations often fail to achieve this kind of growth is due to various factors. Each proponent must be willing to allow critique, which will highlight the fissure that has been missing.

Because we must reside somewhere in the conceptual realm, whatever conceptual absoluteness there is, we will stake our existential self to find composition there. Satisfying for the fissure—or even admitting it—requires an existential disarray until we have found respite in the more comprehensive picture. This is why the process of maturity is filled with misery and setbacks—it requires a leap into existential uncertainty until another version of the conceptual realm is reconstructed.

To make matters worse, the conceptual realm is transitory, proven by its inability to provide lasting existential calm. Once an improved conceptual realm is found, the willingness to formulate another nosedive deteriorates, having previously encountered existential disarray.

In an even worse scenario, those who attempt to continuously seal fissures without a sense of respite, enter into indefinite existential disarray, having lost the ground to maintain composure. This reflects what may be described as a

---

[2] Plato, *Meno*, 81a–86b, circa 380 BCE.

loss of conceptual stability or coherence. Another form of insanity is the perpetual unwillingness to stop the fissures of the conceptual realm until it becomes so dislodged that the very ground of respite can no longer be maintained. In this case, the return becomes more challenging, as there is no developed conceptual framework to return to in order to find conceptual respite.

While in the other form of insanity—with a certain calm from unceasing endeavored improvements—without any conscious work, sanity may begin to find its way, for there is a conceptual ground to rest upon.

Another failure in conversation occurs when participants are unwilling to address each other's fissures. Instead, they engage in dialogue that surfaces these fissures but avoids diving into them, as doing so requires dynamic shifts. A dynamic shift happens when one participant exposes a conceptual fissure, which the other receives and accepts. Once integrated, an innovative conceptual picture forms. This compels the recipient to identify and critique a new fissure—this time in the original critique.

Only after the initial critique is accepted and integrated can the secondary critique be meaningful. Otherwise, the secondary critique is used only to deflect the existential experience that they are unwilling to endure. Moreover, it will not be the accurate fissure, since they cannot recognize such a fissure while their own, unaddressed gap remains unacknowledged. How can one critique a *critique* if they had not understood the initial critique?

Surfacing fissures is a clever way to engage in conversation without dialogue. Without dynamic shifts, there is no existential experience. Yet without existential stimulation, the conversation remains uninhabited. It becomes receptive to external conversations, borrowing existential overtones, while the private experience grows disquieting. Individuals in this situation often turn to public forums to derive stimulation from external interactions, facilitating an indirect yet impactful dynamic shift.

A particularly nuanced example of this dynamic shift arises in intimate relationships. Here, conceptual fissures often go unaddressed until indirectly confronted through surrogate environments. Public forums, for example, can serve as mediating spaces for individuals struggling to resolve private conceptual challenges—acting much like external stimuli that enable subconscious reflection. Sexuality, in this context, reveals itself as a vivid domain where a stable dynamic shift is necessary for full experience. If two parties cannot achieve this shift privately, a third-party observer may facilitate this subconscious change. By observing others who are themselves stimulated, the couple absorbs that experience into their private interaction. This shifts into the universal realm to obtain the necessary conversation, while avoiding it in the conscious or private realm.

One can experience sexual stimulation without a defined dynamic shift. An external observer might find their engagement shaped by personal reflections, which, in turn, influence the dynamics of their conceptual interactions. The individual within the intimate exchange absorbs and reciprocates the external stimulus, forming a cycle of indirect interaction. A significant question is how shifts in perspective occur during conceptual negotiations.

The answer lies in what is intimate to them. This phenomenon underscores a paradoxical dynamic: individuals may unknowingly rely on strangers to mediate subconscious desires, bypassing direct engagement with personal intimacy.

This is internalized as if it were a private exchange. In this way, they enter the universal realm for necessary conversation, yet when presented in their conscious or private realm, they are unwilling to engage with it directly.

Another manner by which conversation is halted is through the exchange of details secondary to existential understanding. These details are unnecessary in raw form and become applicable due to their future promise of existential relevance. Yet even though secondary, they are anchored to the existential realm. A dynamic shift occurs when the dialogue satisfies the missing details, stimulating the subconscious layer of the conversation.

THE CONCEPTUAL LANDSCAPE AND THE TIMING OF ACTION

For instance, in a conversation about directions, there is a sublayer processing the purpose of the destination and its relation to the origin. If a particular road is mentioned, it reflects existential needs—whether at the destination or along the way. This layer is repressed but present. We can focus on the details so intently that the existential layer involuntarily exhibits itself. A detailed conversation about directions may reveal the purpose of the destination and reflect the speaker's current state of life.

Those attempting to avoid this sublayer will continuously shift from one conversation to another so that the dynamic shift of its details will not provoke an existential shift. We can appreciate this readily in a normal conversation about directions, avoiding supplementary notations due to the existential situation about the destination and their state of existence in relation to it—or despite it.

We cannot claim that action is merely an intermediate phase between the conceptual realm and its ongoing development within the stream of life. There are multiple stages in the conceptual landscape, one of which is the *residential phase*—to reside comfortably within the conceptual understanding of the moment.

The second phase involves recognizing conceptual fissures. This marks the beginning of reconstruction, as it requires acknowledging the fallibility of the assumed conceptual realm. Upon this recognition, one becomes receptive to the available fissure.

Thirdly, there is the *integration* of the fissure with the preceding conceptual realm. This phase involves the amelioration of both—the fissure and its former framework—into a newly formed conceptual landscape. This renewed landscape becomes the new housing for existential calm and comfort.

Action is most apparent when one is residing, for in this stage, the conceptual realm is assumed to be the completeness of reality as one knows it. Activity accordingly becomes the mode of transport for human movement. Consider, for example, a situation involving directions. By the conclusion of the conversation, there emerges a new conceptual understanding. The landscape has been enlarged, and there is now a possibility of residing in that security. Consequently, it becomes an interval where material action must take responsibility and follow those movements.

If, upon the journey, the conceptual realm is brought into question, then continuing in the realm of action creates a conflicting state of affairs. There is no need for action when the conceptual realm is itself requesting attention, and it is only in tending to that realm that one may succeed. If one continuously follows a questionable conceptual realm while simultaneously engaging in material activity, the result is action embodying a deteriorating conceptual foundation—each movement pulling in differing directions, contradicting itself from moment to moment.

Still, one may choose to find ground in a questionable conceptual realm without filling in its fissures at that moment. For example, as the journey becomes questioned, one may decide that such a direction is nonetheless the only viable path. For that intermediary period, material action becomes the mode of transport. While reality may seem in question, one can choose at any moment to reside within a given conceptual state—to become a resident of something rather than everything, and thus avoid becoming a nonentity.

The conclusion of any conversation—taken here in its existential sense—is the moment in which activity becomes necessary. During action, the conceptual realm is assumed in its entirety, and any questioning can invoke a departure from necessary motion. For instance, in the mode of work, questioning one's interactions with the task introduces conceptual uncertainty, which may require that the work be paused. This only applies where work has a material manifestation; if the work is purely conceptual, this restriction does not apply, e.g., artists.

How are we to know when a conversation has reached its conclusion? In one sense, the conceptual process may deserve continuous attention. Still, one indicator of conclusion is when one proponent becomes unwilling to proceed.

Another indicator is the material state of either proponent, in which they are unavailable to follow the conceptual landscape and its intended position—for instance, if they are tired. But if both are materially able and existentially willing, what would be the other indicators?

This would be seen in the dynamic shift of either proponent, in which one is unwilling to proceed into more existential disarray, beginning to display inconsistent logic that does not follow a sequential conceptual landscape appropriate for the situation. They may activate a certain defensive behavior in which they seek the conceptual fissure of the other proponent without being receptive to their own fissure which has already been exposed.

Another indicator is emotionally fused aggression, or its subtler forms, which signal the onset or potential escalation of conflict. Instead of being exposed to their own existential state, they may act—again, using the word *act* instead of *converse*—in an attempt to enter the material realm while the conversation is strictly conceptual. This aggression manifests as a transition from conceptual disarray into material activity while still anchored to a conceptual position. At its extreme, aggression becomes occupied material activity without the availability of conversation.

Even in that case, aggression at no time fully detaches from the conceptual realm—for if it did, it would not be aggression but simple material activity or external disruption. Aggression retains conceptual content and intent, but lacks receptivity. At this point, we might say that for material activity undertaken against another to be considered non-aggressive, there must be no conceptual input into its performance. This would be found in a case where conceptual development has been thoroughly mitigated. At the conclusion of that conceptual landscape, one is now free to enact material movements that disrupt other bodies.

In a proper civilization, managing this effectively is to distribute roles accordingly—with the judicial system for the conceptual realm and the military for the material. To expect the same individual to operate conceptually and materially in due time, without fusing the two and triggering aggression to ascend, is too difficult an ask.

From another perspective, aggression can be seen as a sign of unwillingness to follow the conceptual realm to its conclusion, opting instead to leap prematurely into material action. The appropriate time for action comes only after the conceptual landscape has been clarified—when one has chosen a stable ground upon which to existentially rest. However, in the material manifestation of a single social body acting upon another, it is often the case that one is motivated to achieve conceptual refinement rather than selecting a single ground to stand on.

Since material confrontation involves life itself, it is existentially significant. Therefore, in most cases, it is worthwhile to refine the conceptual landscape until no identifiable fissures remain.

ACTION, SACRIFICE AND SERVICE

IN A SENSE, conversation serves as the means by which the material realm is not the sole manifestation of human movement. It facilitates the negotiation of the conceptual realm, allowing it to dominate human activity. As a result, the final form of human action is often mediated at lower levels or through the service of those who remain within that realm. This leads us to another junction—service. These individuals do not reside in the dominant conceptual realm but instead remain grounded in materiality. For them, activity can be performed without consequence, as they are integrated within a conceptual model of lower frequency.

Furthermore, these individuals have the opportunity to undergo a dynamic shift toward those in the conceptual realm. In doing so, they become available for improvement, enabling them to inhabit a more conceptual landscape. This benefits those already within the conceptual realm, as they are often deficient in material activity, which is comprehended as a distraction from their development.

Material activity becomes a significant payoff for the conceptual realm, as it requires individuals to temporarily separate from abstract thought in order to fully engage with materiality. The value of material engagement lies in its unique ability to affect the conceptual realm—something that cannot be fully achieved through abstract thought alone.

This question continues to challenge the conceptual realm and, in doing so, furthers its superior objective. Fewer material excursions are more favorable to the conceptual domain and its preservation. However, when one is compelled to engage more severely with the material, it becomes an opportunity for the conceptual realm to evolve, potentially creating an entirely new form of consciousness.

No individual can be deemed not fit for material activity, as there are at all times conceptual fissures or aspects of consciousness that require revelation. However, these periods of materiality need not be extensive or prolonged. A moderate amount of material action can be effective across a wide domain within the conceptual realm, depending on an individual's developmental stage. An individual's placement within the hierarchy of service is determined by their standing in the conceptual landscape. Correspondingly, their role and performance in service are defined by the extent of their material engagement.

Service becomes a complex arena because providing it to those within an expanded conceptual landscape necessitates a dynamic shift—one that allows individuals to receive a heightened measure of consciousness through their service. This process requires a strict hierarchy of service. At the top are those who remain closely aligned with the conceptual realm, yet still capable of engaging in material manifestation. These individuals would serve the next generation, as they are most justifiable of this measure of consciousness, being more attuned to the conceptual process.

In the age of capitalism, however, the conceptual realm can be severed from monetary concerns. As a result, the hierarchy of service, once aligned with conceptual standing, can be misleading. This disruption can then lead to widespread societal resentment and unfulfillment across various ranks. Individuals with an expanded conceptual capacity may find themselves either without service altogether or confronted with service so complex that it becomes overwhelming. Conversely, those involved in service may receive a prescription of consciousness through their disadvantage but fail to reciprocate with individuals of considerable conceptual depth. Their status is now determined by economic activity, rather than alignment with conceptual order.

BRIDGING CONCEPTUAL AND MATERIAL REALMS

In an attempt to resolve this tension, some may seek to blend material activity with the conceptual realm, bypassing the structured and civilized hierarchy outlined above. They may attempt to carry out material acts while simultaneously engaging with the conceptual realm, as if no degradation occurs in either realm. However, this introduces a significant dilemma: this will reflect the instability of the conceptual, or vice versa. The material jurisdiction, by its very nature, is non-conceptual and therefore adulterated. When the conceptual dominion follows it, it becomes lost to itself.

Contrary to common assumptions, material activity does not effortlessly integrate into one's identity; rather, it requires deliberate alignment with the conceptual framework. Rather, it is a manifestation of the conceptual realm, operating according to the moment dictated by it. When attention is shifted to the material jurisdiction, the conceptual dominion degrades exponentially, preventing the integration of the material action into one's personhood. If one tries to access the conceptual dominion during the performance of a material act, the activity itself becomes inconsistent—an instability that then reverberates back into the conceptual realm. Following a material action, the preceding conceptual realm becomes available once again, marking an additional expense of action.

Part II – Intimacy, Power, and Persona

DIALOGUE AND NARRATIVE

THE REPRESENTATION of internal dialogue cannot be performed in any other fashion than as a descriptive formulation of its process. We could perform the narrative arc, but we cannot provide details of its process, because the quality of displaying a narrative arc is that it overlooks the internal thoroughfare which follows a logical sequence of dialogue. A conversation may have a narrative arc structure that is noticed but can be ignored—until another narrative is revealed. This process is, in theory, indefinite.

One may follow the narrative arc of conversation and acknowledge when to lead based upon it. However, in certain terms, this is a betrayal of the dialogue itself. As the dialogue progresses, narrative structures are revealed—but not in the aspects of the dialogue itself. The dialogue moves according to the existential movement of each proponent, which is not a decision made by any narrative structure. Each person determines where the dialogue leads, and a new narrative will emerge according to this movement.

Many will naturally follow the narrative presenting itself in the moment in order to guard against a failed submersion into existential attachment. However, this protective mechanism also disrupts the dialogue itself, as one becomes focused on a manifestation of the dialogue rather than its content. By ignoring the narrative arc, one becomes less protected—but gains the ability to develop within the dialogue and follow its sequence, whether it fails or succeeds.

Failure must be allowed its rightful manifestation, because the developed state that leads to it is the authentic work—prior to the dialogue. Once the dialogue takes place, one cannot reside in any domicile of protection. If failure is the intended object, they must existentially attach to whatever that object is. Greater than the failure of existential submersion is the avoidance of it, because such avoidance produces a lack of individuation in dialogue—dialogue that is ruled solely by a connection to a narrative arc, one that can be whirled in any direction by the psyche. Moreover, the development of personhood is most deeply motivated by the existential plunge, which has a way of naturally instructing the psyche in constructing a more elaborate structure for future engagement.

At the same time, the experience of existential loss can motivate a more intricate protective mechanism. The only protection worthwhile to personhood is a more elaborate internal structure—one that can follow a sequence, risk failures, and still hold the possibility of success by virtue of having a developed state. That immersement requires a nosedive unencumbered by the failures of the past, with allegiance to a novel selfhood that will perform however it must. A protective measure focused on prior mistakes will wedge new developments from being included in the immersement, ensuring failure—particularly if that protective measure continually disrupts all movement.

Dialogue differs from narrative in that it does not move in a direction that accounts for past, present, and future. It follows an intellectual sequence, where conversation moves forward or becomes halted for reasons outside its own process. We might say that one's internal dialogue shifts due to the narrative, but we cannot follow that dialogue without abandoning the narrative structure.

In fact, entering into a narrative structure requires dialogue—and leaving it materializes the same way. We participate in a new story because internal and external dialogues led us there. Prior to the story, there was a narrative—but it is not included in the arc. The narrative structure concludes when dialogue renders the story uninteresting. That loss of interest arises from internal dialogue, not from the narrative arc itself. This is why we can add an additional arc when it seems fit—because dialogue seeks to re-enter a familiar pattern.

To further explore this tension between dialogue and narrative, consider the following detail on contemptable dialogue and narrative. We can perceive each piece of dialogue as a very short narrative structure, to which the other proponent responds with another narrative structure. By the end of the dialogue, it will have been the recipient of numerous small narrative arcs.

This may resemble a normal narrative, with one caveat: in each intermission, there is a loss of connection to the previous narrative in order for the new one to take hold. Though they are threaded by a logical sequence, a microscopic examination reveals logical fissures.

For instance, the previous sentence discussed the space between two narrative structures. The next sentence went on to show how they are connected. However, a closer review of the logic in the transition reveals breaches. I first emphasized separation, then followed with a notion of continuity, implying a lack of separation.

One might argue that the first perspective was meant to provide a backdrop of availability upon which the next sentence attempted to build—acknowledging that space remains. Still, this does not fully explain the connection between the clauses. The explanation served each part individually, but not the relation itself.

We could explore this relationship further, but we are ultimately forced to admit that there is no absolute logical continuity—only narratives that align within a certain logic, one that retains fissures. Had we aimed for perfect logical continuity, we would have lost the sense of logicality and, surely, its narrative structure.

Dialogue is evidence of existential attachment and disengagement to narrative structures which endure. It cannot persist without being deeply connected to existential absolutism, which offers the highest regard for information. A broad narrative arc, such as "history repeats itself," will not serve as a valid component of streamlined dialogue. Just as we might say that this moment in the dialogue will repeat itself, so too might we say another will. The broad narrative arc can be applied to any detail—it can serve as the rising action or the climax, depending on where we choose to place our focus.

MANIPULATION AND RESPONSE

THE REATTACHMENT can be done unceremoniously, as is common for those with a strong identity in their practice of weaving their material through abrupt measures of systematic manipulation. The difficulty is that coerced conversation is not a reciprocity of a shared conceptual realm, but rather singular, parallel lines of thought. The one who is weaving the material is basing themselves on a continued consideration without the availability to dynamically change.

They must establish a conversation that integrates their material. While this might appear natural—as though the conceptual realm organically facilitated it, the reciprocation of that material is not genuinely integrated into the psyche. It does not reflect a true dynamic exchange. The psyche is self-aware of the containments that preceded the arrival of this material. It recognizes that it did not seek such material as a necessity for the conceptual realm. There was no fissure waiting to be resolved—no conceptual void that had found its proper outlet.

Since the material being manipulated consists of universal themes that are not part of the sociality, an individual may, through a method, reinvigorate a conscious fissure that was not previously there. However, the psyche is even aware of this: it acknowledges that the fissure was invigorated against sociality. While normal exchange leaves one affixed in a conscious fissure with a lineage of events that eventually covers the space through rigorous existential development, in this case, the fissure is immediately filled with its antidote. Even without the antidote, upon returning to the sociality—which has not found this conscious fissure to be a self-conscious experience—they will lose its sense over time.

This is why there is no delay between the individual becoming aware of the new fissure and the immediate process of filling it. Had they waited, the social realm would have placated the newly formed self-consciousness, and the fissure would be existentially forgotten. Once the fissure is filled, the individual becomes a part of these universal themes, even if they need not know it. However, having occurred, they can still provide an adjacent understanding to societal universal themes, which will realign themselves with sociality.

Until that moment arises, they are dutifully bound to two conceptual realms: one personal and the other, social. Having found a universal order that is not being exposed within the societal realm may cause the individual to consider departing its haven and partaking wholly in the realm that contains new models. This, however, works against personhood—which is a being of sociality—by then segregating them within a community of universal themes.

When returning to sociality, which is inevitable, they will either hurriedly interact with resentful disruption or they will lose the realm they are building in their private domain—until, that is, they parallel the private universal themes with sociality. Upon aligning developed universal themes with the broader social framework, these themes transition from isolated constructs to universally relevant concepts. They have already found an outline that grants permission for private universal themes to be on par with the congruent sociality.

The private universal themes will become a kind of secondary tier of observation for sociality and will be treated as a tool for the institutionalized system. This means that although they initially sought the secluded universal themes for their own sake—namely, the first tier of observation—they are now required to be demoted to the second tier, serving only as a method for absolute sociality. When they continue to interact with the secluded community, it will be for methodological reasons in maintaining their access to sociality.

Additionally, whatever those universal themes may be, they will be approached from the vantage point of the already institutionalized theme, of which they are merely an enhancement. Thus, the interaction becomes institutionalized even though the themes themselves are not. If they demonstrate any kind of predisposed attachment to these second-tier themes, they will lose the institutionalized theme. They will also reveal an underdeveloped conceptual realm—espousing socially accepted themes, but with an underlying attachment to the second-tier themes. This will render their ideas convoluted, shaped by an outline that is neither accepted nor of interest to others.

Likewise, conversing with the second-tier community while demonstrating societal universal themes will introduce a preponderance of sociality, thereby diluting the purity of isolation and development.

This differs from the voluntary interaction of individuals who recognize others as conveying certain material and request to engage with it. In that case, they become representations of the material, making it a willed interaction. Yet, it can be said that those who practice the infusion of conversation with their respective material will not find respite in the reciprocity of such interaction. Ironically, they sense that they are being used—not for conceptual dynamics (which they are already unwilling to partake in)—but as representations of what another individual is already seeking.

In such a sense, they become self-conscious of their behavior—of utilizing the dynamic for their material's validation in the societal universal exchange.

MIRROR DYNAMICS IN RELATIONSHIPS

ADVANCED SOCIAL BEINGS interact through the biological reflection of external individuals, who act as mirrors to validate the precedent of existence. Within these interactions, each person is expected to enact a reflection earnest of the reciprocity of the moment.

Let us begin—perhaps unfairly—by focusing on a specific characteristic within relationships: manipulation. Each participant in a manipulative exchange operates within an expected domain, embodying who they are presumed to be. This expectation stems from biological mirroring. Without it, the individual ceases to function as a mirror and becomes an arbitrary organism—devoid of internal reflection, and therefore unfit for consciousness. What is valuable to humans are the internal data points they behold; anything external to those points lacks inherent interest. We find something "interesting" only when it brings about interconnection.

This expectation exists within a loosely defined domain—vague in its parameters, yet maintaining a critical boundary common to all: it must exist at a certain existential depth. Individuals are not expected to remain on the surface, nor to descend into deeper, already-claimed existential territory.

Territory is defined by claims or accepted parameters—both internal and external. If the boundary is extended too far, it loses stability; if condensed, it transforms into something else entirely. Consider a servant's quarters, for example: even when housed within elaborate estates, they remain a distinct entity.

An individual's defined parameters are shaped by prior interactions. When one fails to maintain their expected existential ground, they seek to renegotiate it. While biological reflection can offer valuable overlays of personhood, excessive widening makes that reflection incoherent. At its limit, reflection loses its form, and validation is no longer possible.

Take, for instance, the interaction between elites and sub-elites. The elite does not experience a full biological reflection. The exchange becomes coarse unless the elite chooses to use the sub-elite as a reminder of some inherent part of themselves. In that case, the reflection may represent only a single *organ*—valuable in certain contexts, but insufficient for reflecting the whole organism.

Perfect mirroring—where neither party expanses—yields no insight. In such cases, assumptions are mutually shared and unchallenged. The reflection appears again as a single fragment, requiring interaction with components of personhood that do not constitute the complete picture. Reflecting on one fragment comes at the expense of the entire organism, a trade-off that may, in some cases, be worthwhile.

At this stage of perfected mirroring, the biological reflection ceases to offer novelty. The psyche then creates a dramatic wedge, coercing elasticity through material changes. Rather than the conceptual realm evolving naturally, sentiment is driven materially. Speech and behavior are used to introduce troubling sentiments into the reflection between individuals, forcing expansion. When others appear to interrupt the harmony, they expose a point of reflection per a perceived error.

Because this perceived error can appear in any biological reflection—so long as it aligns with expected form—it can be brought to awareness. Gossip, though disruptive, can be a tool to raise awareness of conceptual vulnerabilities. But gossip behaves differently when one is required to reflect upon themselves and to those who reflect upon them. Nature—or reality—is the foundation of reflection, while gossip becomes its conscious performance. In a society that values self-awareness and relational integrity, gossip is held in high regard. Indeed, gossip thrives where consciousness flows freely.

In environments of low consciousness, gossip is unconnected—it tries to expose vulnerabilities in what lacks vitality. Where consciousness is highest, gossip is most respected, transforming vulnerability into interest through leverage. The subject of gossip may either rise to the social (and existential) demand, resent the exposure, or embrace shame as an embodiment of vulnerability.

All wrongdoing can be understood through this framework. The key distinction lies in whether vulnerabilities are consciously acknowledged. Friendships, for example, subtly explore those vulnerabilities to encourage growth within the dynamic. Gossip drives this to the extreme, but it also existentially binds the gossiper to the recipient. In exposing disparity, the gossiper aligns themselves through reflection. Even with dubious intent, this act is—psychically—the inmost form of attachment.

Vulnerability exposed by gossip cannot be dismissed. It demands entry into a new realm of existential uncertainty. Even if the same existential space is revisited, social exposure compels immediate change. Most are uncomfortable being inserted into existential chaos and consequently adopt defensive mechanisms.

They may redirect this disruption toward the instigator, believing that shared discomfort will balance the dynamic and create a new domain of comfort. Yet often, they are already in confusion—simply avoiding it in their private lives.

The public realm externalizes that vulnerability, making it an object of shared interaction. A private individual cannot enjoy the privilege of scandal—they are shielded from both such potential and its vulnerabilities. While this should not be permissible in social structures, privatization allows one to live with unexamined vulnerabilities, avoiding existential engagement. Once publicly exposed, the social world treats the individual as real—as someone with whom they can authentically interact with. The cost of actualization is that all aspects, especially vulnerabilities, are now open to attention. Shame arises not from failure, but from having avoided the existential depth that such an exposure demands.

If the other party rejects renegotiated terms, the relationship exits its feedback loop. Material may still be exchanged, but biological mirroring ceases. One may mirror an animal and draw insights, but this is not true biological mirroring—it remains conceptual. A biological mirror must act consciously and in the expected ways.

Thus, we must distinguish between ongoing biological representation and a departed mirror of specific traits. When elites engage with sub-elites, they may recall aspects of themselves—but this is memory, not reflection. One cannot mirror solitary fragments of self; the ego does remain whole. The only way to mirror a part is to construct a contextual interaction that connects the ego to its former self through another.

The natural form of that mirror is memory, because the opposing party does not serve as the perfect reflection of the moment. Interacting with memory means using the other to reinvigorate a part of oneself, rather than engaging with the present moment. This requires continuous intellectual effort, as it is not a natural form of interaction, and one cannot prove themselves as such in relationships. It is only an effort to periodically engage with pieces of oneself, but eventually, a proper biological representation will occur when the reflection is received in the wholeness of the individual in front of them.

If the other fails to mirror an exaggerated psyche, they diminish in value. Thus, an elite who remains elongated among sub-elites, without a contextual bridge to small parts of themselves, risks becoming sub-elite.

This scarcity of mirror-like relationships in adulthood—outside of family—reflects maturity. Family provides the clearest reflection of present existential states. Even if it does not reflect full personhood, what is reflected is invariably tied to the whole. The family functions as a singular extension of the self, offering a unique mirror. Other relationships require bridging between personhood and the aspects that bring vitality.

This is the essence of maturity: arriving at a stage where few people mirror the wholeness of one's being. Maturity introduces nuance, which is lost in absolute relationships. The child, in contrast, thrives in such relationships because they need a direct mirror to explore the form of their identity. They lack the defenses of maturity and thus rely on raw reflection. That's why maturity often returns to memory—to revisit those primary mirrors that shaped the present self.

To lament adulthood as the loss of mirroring relationships is to voice the loneliness of a person who has completed their inner structure. It is indeed lonely—but that is the nature of maturity. Loneliness signals the loss of interactive components, though they can be re-accessed through mirrors of lost elements.

Maturity has reached a point where it cannot revert to the immature mirror but still lacks the full realization of its maturity. While it cannot use these relationships to regress to childhood, it can utilize them to address the aspects of itself that cause isolation. However, prolonged exposure to any one individual will bring an existential attachment to the wholeness of personhood. The familial body, for example, can cause one to regress to a part of themselves but will certainly not threaten to revert to an immature version.

The non-familial mirror can place one at the existential behest of being mirrored, regardless of any progress made by the individual. The worst-case scenario for the familial body is when it mirrors only a fragment of the self at the expense of the whole; it can be corrected through broader reflection. For example, an adult may begin to think like their child, but the psyche can trace a path back to mature personhood. Conversely, if an elite remains among sub-elites and mirrors their traits for too long, they lose their wholeness. Returning from this state requires serious intellectual work—like a fiction writer recovering their identity after immersion in a subculture.

We, in turn, read such fiction because we all seek that same retrieval of personhood, which is lost through exposure to the limited mirror of enduring relationships. This plot is often the most intriguing in fiction books, which differ from films in that fiction allows a detailed approach to exploring this existential journey. Film, by contrast, cannot provide the same depth due to its reliance on external action over internal dialogue. Interpersonal exchanges inevitably scale up to group-level processes, as explored in the next section.

STAGES OF GROUP FORMATION

WE WILL REVIEW the necessity of sociality, to which much information about the workings of the social mechanism manifests for the psyche apparatus. If we find a tendency in the system where sociality changes according to the maturity level, then we can identify the aspects of differentiation.

We notice that group sociality is a normal occurrence until a certain age, after which there is a buffer range—agreed upon by social custom—followed by a pace of maturity where group sociality becomes burdensome to the social system. These ages change with the era, so we must adhere to generalities and agree that the three stages do occur: [1] Normal social groupings. [2] A gray zone where transition is expected. [3] A final stage where social settings are expected to disallow group sociality.

We may question the shift in maturity where social groupings transform from a method of sociality to a point where the psyche advances beyond that. Let us examine the objective of social groupings in this context, as it appears that a set of benefits becomes obsolete with the advancement of age and psyche development.

The first of these benefits is internal dialogue. When this dialogue has not yet matured, individuals require social groupings to mirror each other and activate that internal process. As maturity develops, the psyche becomes capable of providing a coherent and advanced internal dialogue—one that no longer necessitates group sociality.

This explains why there is no taboo regarding social groupings at any age when the material being enhanced belongs to a contextual framework. By 'contextual framework,' we refer to institutions of any kind—habitats that foster group sociality because individuals have not yet advanced their internal dialogue enough to process the complexity of the institution. For instance, universities present complex information that necessitates group sociality, even for those who have matured socially outside such settings.

However, when advancement does occur, the individual within the university requires a maturity beyond that sociality, for the variety of such conversation has already been internalized. When a professor finds themselves in need of sociality, we may question their level of maturity or intentions, for they should have already incorporated that information into their internal biology. There are only two likely reasons for continued group sociality in such cases: [1] They did not advance according to the traditional stages, [2] They retain contextual objectives that are not aligned with normal sociality.

The primary intention, then, would be to provide a teaching environment that functions best in a group setting. The professor, in this case, would not engage in the same manner but would remain reserved, enabling group sociality without becoming an existential link in it. This dynamic may fill a gap in their own level of advancement or engage innocent layers of their developing psyche.

For example, when a parent interacts with a child, they may seek to reconnect with the innocence they have lost, using the interaction to balance their own maturity with a sense of nostalgia. Instead, the parent seeks such innocence through a contextual perspective. They do not truly wish to become innocent again, but rather to be reminded of it. This approach allows them to become better-rounded in their maturity.

Whether we are speaking of the professor or the parent, the social grouping is not for existential exchange but for contextual or interactive resolutions that are not existentially threatening to them. They may engage with students to survey the realities of new generational interpretations, but this interaction is through an aspect of their psyche, not with the individual student themselves.

Regardless of maturity level, the internal advancement will always retain a vulnerability—a system biased to itself—requiring incremental engagements with sociality to maintain alignment with the external sequence to which all psyche material should be anchored. This form of sociality could be a simple remark or even a brush with a stranger.[3] The point is to have a reference of sociality that can be expanded and eventually internalized by an external attachment.

This leads us to the second benefit of social groupings: providing the externality necessary at any level of maturity. The difference between stages of maturity lies in the amount of externality required to both inform and regulate the internal psyche, bridging the internal and external realms accordingly.

In earlier stages of maturity, direct sociality is more essential because individuals are less adapted to engaging with the external world independently. The internal system is not yet advanced, so external information is poorly received, requiring a greater volume of it to have the intended effect.

As the internal system develops, external information is more easily incorporated and requires less direct interaction. Nevertheless, direct sociality is invariably necessary, as the

---

[3] Walt Whitman, *To a Stranger* as part of *Leaves of Grass*, (1860).

psyche prerequisites a continual stream of external data to construct and maintain an adequate model of reality. This cannot be provided by the passive presence of others—it must come from meaningful interaction.

For example, a brief interaction with a brush of a stranger. The brush of a stranger provides direct interaction, through which the realm of sophistication that has been interacted becomes the setting for the rest of the information.

The psyche cannot include a phrase of externality and permeate its substance throughout, for the condition that internality will recognize such is a process of permeation as an internal mechanism.

In this context, the only difference between maturity and immaturity is the amount of direct interaction with external substance versus the provided indirect interactions of externality, with only a small amount of direct interaction to corroborate social validation. As the advanced psyche interacts with the external realm, even though it relies on an internal mechanism for its interaction, by allowing a vulnerability of information (which the psyche is not imposing on the external realm but allowing the external realm to do to the psyche), then the information will be considered forms of externality. The reason for more direct validation is for the purpose of humanistic corroboration, which intervenes to address the aspect of questioning genuine externality, which has not been experienced thus far, for the most genuine is considered direct social connection.

The reason direct sociality is considered most genuine is that childhood advancement accrued from that domain. Psyche development relies on the modeling of humanistic endeavors, which then become a portal to personify the external realm. Even though the external realm is the ground of most information material, it is the dynamic interaction of that preliminary model that allows for that interaction. The caveat of this realm is that the personification is formalized with a certain internality, as can be said for direct humanistic connection. For this reason, there will always be a disparity between internality and externality. The greatest achievement of maturity is to bridge **these** realms as seamlessly as possible, without compromising each of them.

When we observe a group of adults engaged in sociality without a clear contextual basis, we often assume it is disconnected from normal social behavior. The only exception is familial grouping, which has advantages not seen elsewhere. The family is a form of biological refraction, where individuals partake in aspects of their existential components, spread out in the form of external members.

VALUING ATTENTION

ONE OF THE KEY elements that ensures continual progression along the spectrum of consciousness development is the cost—or expense—of each exposure. If one can anticipate that by engaging with a particular exposure, they will emerge on the other side with a heightened degree of awareness, they must also be prepared to submit to the demands of that realm. In essence, they become the forfeiture to the endeavor of consciousness, often realizing in hindsight that the initial exposure may not have been a value of the cost.

This is why economic output becomes such a prevalent metric: it offers tangible evidence of the cost-effectiveness of each cognitive or experiential investment, assigning a value to the application of significance to any given exposure. A lower economic standard can, in this context, act as a filler for a weakened or diminished state of consciousness—representing the social expense of consciousness exposure. Because of this relationship, we often observe a parallel between economic direction and levels of consciousness. The rewards and expenses of certain involvements then structure a lifestyle that either enables or inhibits participation in the proper stages or permutations of development.

In more elaborate terms, this means that a socially aware cognition recognizes how their environment offers specific exposures, which may become obsolete or overwhelmed by more elevated exposures available beyond that realm. Thus, one learns to preserve or generate their exposure through various methods, aiming to facilitate the form of experiential appropriation most aligned with their developmental sequence.

However, regardless of the final state one attains, there will continually exist a higher substrate of consciousness. One must be willing to accept the level of awareness accessible to them at any given time, while acknowledging that full dissemination of that awareness only occurs through exposure to its more refined realms.

This raises a fundamental question of metrics: If there exists an uppermost form of consciousness, why not encourage individuals to practice participation in that domain from the outset? Doing so would reduce the risk of being destabilized by the expenditure of lesser exposures. Even if one does temporarily descend into a lower tier of consciousness, they are not absent; rather, they are merely displaced from the ideal sequence. Reacquainting themselves with the uppermost realm would allow them to realign with the proper path of conscious evolution.

TRADING EXPOSURE

THERE IS A PROCESS of exchange within sociality, and its purpose is to propose either sentimental value in the direction of consciousness or interactivity as the foundation of a consciousness hierarchy. There is no other reason for social exchange other than to perform the reciprocity of these two elements. One might extract from sociality a representational value, which is another form of conscious substance, or they might find validation, which is another form of interactivity. But for the sake of understanding, we have these two polar opposites, which remain at the extremes, and to which we can define both hostile exchanges as well as the most vital ones.

For a conscious substance that requires interactivity, there is nothing more vital than exchange. For an interactive bubble, there is no primacy other than the reception of conscious substance to deter its secluded process.

In a high-volume interactive environment, it is likely that exchange will take place significantly enough to provide the sensible exchanges that give it conscious substance. However, this is also the most contentious form of exchange, as it allows for the unraveling of the secluded system. In this way, a hostile exchange can be determined by the extreme to which the exchange has reached a tipping point, making it so vital that it raises the sentiment of unmasking.

The same dynamic occurs in an individual or environment that retains too much conscious substance, where interactivity becomes vital but also hostile, as it disrupts the system and demands an itemization of consciousness to allow for interactivity. However, this is usually less the case because consciousness, when functioning normally, relies on representational value—a form of interactivity that works to give credence to a consciousness hierarchy.

It is possible, though, that one can deviate from a proper consciousness system, in which case, anything that proposes an imbalance of interactivity and possessiveness will be considered hostile and disruptive.

We can even define every hostile social exchange as either an interactive obsession, where the vitalness of exchange is not allowed its proper course, or consciousness adherence, where the inclusion of lower systemic aspects is seen as hostile. This critique is often embodied by the adolescence stage, who provide a streamlined proposal that the exchange process is oppressive in either direction. In doing so, they regulate and control that exchange by finding reclusiveness in the claimants of interactivity or by confronting the consciousness oversight that neglects such interactivity.

The adolescence stage embodies this critique because it is most attuned to the exchange value and process. With such sensitivity, they correct perceived errors and disrupt the societal system that veers too far in a single direction. This is not universal, as parental or political systems may regulate their psyche, causing them to ignore this sensitivity and instead follow a premediated societal process. The political front can present to adolescents a mechanism for following a critique alongside their regulation, turning them into avatars of the state rather than allowing them to independently recognize the failed exchange.

What is often perceived is that the political system will claim the right to critique that exchange with an already formulated proposal, so that the adolescent will take up the cause as if it were their personal hostility. It is usually the case that what is assumed to be an imbalance of social exchange by a political system is frequently the opposite of the real process in the social setting, for the reason that the political body has an objective that is indifferent to real social exchange. In fact, true social exchange cannot be an objective of the political body, as it cannot concern itself with personal sentimentality, only simulated hostility that lacks concern for individuality.

When we observe a society where adolescence can critique social exchange based on their personal sensitivity—different from one another—we can determine that such a society is progressing without a major decline through political or parental control. However, the critique of adolescence may also become so drastic that they resort to reclusivity, demonstrating an imbalance in which they fail to mediate and voice a solution for healing between exchanges. In their reclusivity, they merely protect their own process from enduring the imbalance of exchange, unable to offset the process. This is more prevalent in the interactive fixation, where the reclusivity of adolescence prevents them from finding mediation with consciousness attachment. Every attempt to engage only deepens their isolation within the enclave of interactivity.

This is also the case for consciousness adherence, where the interactivity proposed by adolescence is neglected or ignored to the extent that they must seek more and more interactivity to generate substantial reciprocity between exchanges. However, the consciousness system is structured in a way that exchange is repeatedly available, though it requires unpretentiousness to engage with it in its proper format. This accessibility may be hindered, and the critique becomes more about interactivity in which it is at a closer pace to conscious musing.

ADOLESCENT CRITIQUE OF SOCIAL EXCHANGE SYSTEMS

The adolescent critique can be questioned: is it a proposal for interactivity to enable exchange, or for interactivity that disrupts the flow of consciousness? Perhaps it is hostility toward a lack of inclusion within the consciousness system. If it is hostility, the critique becomes a disruptive force, attempting to offset the imbalance by becoming outcasts. With interactivity, they will disrupt the consciousness system for the mere sake of revenge.

This is the severe manifestation of a critique, in which, in the hope of offsetting the exchange, they will proceed to become outcasts who are mere avatars of disruption rather than proponents of interactivity. This is usually due to the complexity required for the exchange between interactivity and consciousness, and by failed example, they begin to become hostile in their interactivity, only to cause further separation from the possibility of social exchange.

The reclusiveness seen on the other side of the coin arises because the critique of consciousness imbalanced within interactive environments usually comes at the expense of consciousness itself. As the exchange becomes off-balance, the individual or group will need to become more interactive, only to follow the exchange. Rather than becoming a benign critique, adolescence often chooses the reclusive path, waiting for moments of conscious engagement while separating themselves from the exchange altogether.

This is a valid method for addressing the imbalance of exchange. Instead of lowering themselves to an unnecessary interactive state, the individual with conscious prowess internalizes to a realm that does not agree with this exchange. Much like how the consciousness system tends to ignore the proposed interactivity with hostility, they proceed to recluse themselves from engagement, as if the exchange is not occurring or has no social value. The neglect can become so reclusive that it can offset the imbalance simply by not agreeing to the social exchange itself.

We notice that in a consciousness environment, social exchange provides representational value. This means that the reciprocity is not for the interaction between individuals but for how they represent the consciousness system. Individuals become agents of the environment, which expresses sentimental value. The social exchange functions to streamline consciousness into an individualized format. The interactivity that naturally ruminates between sociality forms the basis of consciousness representation, but instead of interacting as distinct social individuals, they imbue the environment with their expressive interactivity so that others can attach not to their individuality, but to the repurposed interaction for social exchange.

There is no expected reciprocity between individuals, but between the representational value of individuals that is sourced in their interactivity. The manner in which one engages with consciousness, where they base a certain interaction of their individual alongside the manner it manifests in the system of representation.

Suffice it to say that social exchange is one where interactivity is mediated by a representational system, placed at the service of public consumption. This is why there is no distinct social exchange in a consciousness system: the sociality is based on representation, and individuals are mere avatars of an environment for individual exchange.

To perceive the consciousness system properly, it is merely a conglomerate of differing substance points meant for the interaction of individuals through their internality. However, to avoid becoming isolated from the environment, there are micro-exchanges that proceed away from the general interaction, providing grounded sociality. These are direct interactions, even if they cannot be considered voiced or actualized interactivity. When direct social exchange is actualized, the proper course is not one of interactivity, for this would detach from the consciousness stream and enter a realm of interactivity. This may be necessary at times, but for engagement with consciousness, it is not.

If one were to deal with the interactive experience to such an extent, it would require contextual oversight, in which the interactions are merely provisions for research on specific embodied topics that are unavailable in the general formation of non-direct social exchange.

The reason the matter is non-direct is that it allows all individual interactions to truly become environmental. Just as nature and its cohort provide the substance of interaction, rather than personal social beings, this form of exchange allows for a certain social access without disrupting the flow of consciousness. Sociality is inherently an adversary of consciousness: the latter is exposing and streamlined, while the former is distinctive and differentiative. We can even say that any form of social exchange, even in a representational format, is a measure of interactivity alongside the continuum of consciousness.

While interactivity is repurposed to avoid disturbing the individual's conscious process, it still remains as a backdrop. There is still a dynamic to analyze between two individuals, though the agreement of this dynamic is mediated by the environment rather than by social beings themselves. The dormant dynamic of direct interactivity can come to fruition if the direction toward interactivity is taken.

We could argue that in each environment, the social exchange unique to its parameters will be considered redundant. For the streamline of consciousness, the sociality that surrounds and represents itself is not all necessary. The continual exchanges are merely pivot points in the flow of consciousness. How many are required to continue without grievance?

Furthermore, in interactive domains, all sociality serves as validation or anti-validation of the premise, and there cannot be sociality otherwise. Therefore, it would be considered redundant because the validation does not need to be endured continuously—just reaffirmed at intervals.

However, in both cases the opposite social exchange is certainly not considered redundant. In the stream of consciousness, any arising interactivity is seen both as disruptive and necessary in the current system, revitalizing it with the reception of conscious substance. Similarly, the interactive domain awaits the social exchange that provides nuance to the consciousness system, as this is their vitalization and would regenerate their system.

Part III – Dynamics of Potential

POTENTIAL: INTERNAL VS. EXTERNAL

THERE ARE TWO ELEMENTS that are linked, through which we can decipher and understand both the success and the disruptions in associations between individuals. To be precise, there is no possibility of potential arising without a form of sociality—whether grounded in a present locale, a nostalgic historical precedent, an imaginative realm, or any other facilitation that provides a sociality from which potential can emerge. Potential that ascends without sociality is considered disruptive to personhood and surrounding environment.

It would be more precise to conceive of potential as a sociological constraint—one that adheres to its parameters as it evolves. In reality, potential represents the next interval in the evolution of a given process. Great potential encompasses all that precedes it while not straying too headlong so as to lose the spectrum from which it originates. Therefore, the constraints of potential are twofold: [1] first, the broad aspect of the sociality from which it stems; and [2] second, the retention of progress that includes all preceding models, leaving none behind in the path forward.

When potential does not include aspects of the surrounding sociality from which it claims to ascend, we may consider it an abomination—in the sense that it possesses substance but lacks a clear lineage to that from which it emerges. There is no identifiable connection between the potential and the sociality, and we cannot discern which aspects of sociality provided its platform. It is as if the potential stands alone, sprouting beyond the sphere of realistic social influence—yet it still manages to evoke a sense of attachment, as it is an encapsulation of potential of something, or of an environment, to which it can somewhat be paralleled.

The second form of disrupted sociality occurs when succession moves forward without adequate inclusion of the past. This resembles potential that ascends from an unrealistic sociality—including, for example, historical or utopian precedents—but in this case, it is more grounded in the framework of potential itself. There is no imaginative leap; rather, there is fidelity to the realistic sense of sociality, yet a failure to account for its full spectrum—thus limiting the progression. Even though the focus remains on potential and its ascendance from sociality, foundational layers of that sociality are forgotten or neglected in pursuit of a goal.

There is no imagined sociality here—the core tenets are retained in the next model or expression of potential—but not the complete history that should accompany it. Certainly, it is not consistently possible to include every element of the past; doing so could, in fact, hinder proper evolution. Every form of sociality contains its shadows, and a focus on incorporating these shadows may go so far as to disrupt future potential. Therefore, managing the parameters of succession—so that they include, but do not over-include—is a nuanced task. It is achievable only when enough of the sociality retains itself for its future period. Having defined the constraints and lineage of potential, we now examine how such potential becomes actualized or remains latent.

POTENTIAL PROCESSES (ACTUAL VS. LATENT)

Now let's cover the degrees to which sociality is a formation of clarity—one that has the complete attention of the social sphere and market exchange. This is top-tier sociality, where the movement of the global conversation culminates, all the while *necessity* has led to this interval. Beside the evolution toward this specific sociality, there is also the matter of the current tension, which stands as the prevailing sentiment for moving forward. We can define this as the global conversation or the global necessity, in which every participant pursues to engage with some degree of relevance.

It is no surprise, then, that the potential emerging from this sociality is considered the highest form of potential. When the base is a fully developed social formation, the potential that can arise from such is of a paramount level. Therefore, the highest base of sociality is typically afforded the market exchange of similar distinction and is the container of economic attention.

Once we remove ourselves from the sociality of peak performance, we begin to understand the many levels underneath. At the lowest echelons of sociality is the family unit, which is the most domesticated form of unique sociality. Certainly, there are more domesticated groupings—perhaps cult-like in nature—but for the sake of universality in this discussion, we'll consider the domestication represented in the family unit as the local form of sociality that is most removed from big levels of sociality.

We can say that potential arising from the family body is of the lowest proportion, simply because it originates from a low form of sociality. In more concrete terms, potential stemming from individual manifestations is not as saturated as that which emerges from major social formations. The larger the degree of sociality plus its more influential stature, the greater the formation of potential.

Potential may appear to ascend from the limited sociality of the family body, but this is only part of the picture. In reality, individuals are shaped by a broader set of environmental influences—many of which occur indirectly through social participation beyond the domestic sphere. While it's true they may emerge from a family-based sociality, which is not the only contributing factor to the manifestation of their potential.

We can say they are characters of sociality pertaining to the environment rather than of the family body—unless it is clear that the ascendancy was based on that family body's sociality. For instance, a royal family or a celebrated lineage, in which, if one were to gain a certain level of potential, we proclaim such ascendancy to be based on the sociality of the family body.

However, in the case of a representational family body, they are already a detail in the broader sociality of the environment rather than a unit of domestication. So it is not an ascendancy of a family body per se, to which they are mere representations of a larger scheme of sociality. Still, we can say that the ascendency is both influenced by the family body and by the environmental aspects that have allowed their public profile to take effect.

This is where we reach the difficulty identified in historical research: it is rather easy to re-identify an encapsulation of potential as an ascendancy of a formalized sociality that is altered than the one proclaimed. Every individual both ascended from their familial bod, their identity structure, liminal social groupings, their state, their environment, and other such influential measures.

Each of these aspects can claim itself as the sociality that provided for that ascendancy. Yet, what is interesting about these historical proclamations is that it is the case that the significance of that potential is based on a global or major environmental sociality. So the reference point in which we study the ascendency of potential is negated in order to proclaim a liminal sociality.

We don't see the reverse—where there is no ascendancy on the global sphere, yet liminal social groupings claim the rights of that potential. For it is only considered a major degree of potential when it had already ascended from environmental aspects.

However, environmental ascendancy can either be based on influential measures that have been taken vis-à-vis the potential and environment, or it can be an environmental attention toward a privatization that is found to be worthwhile for ascendency. Meaning: is it the environment that has sought out the potential that lay dormant (and would remain dormant without discovery), or is it an encapsulation of potential that had arisen based on a reciprocal relationship between environmental influence and individual propriety?

When it is the latter, there's no ability to proclaim any other sociality than the all-inclusive environmental influence—for it was and is the concurring relationship that has led to the ascendency of potential. We could make a claim for translational elements and other preliminary stages that allowed for such ascendency, but we would not be accurate to the wholesome nature of the current relationship, which has surpassed foundational elements.

If it is the former, then we do have the ability to proclaim that the potential was an ascendency from liminal sociality— because it has not participated in a direct relationship with the wholesome environmental aspects, but was rather discovered by them. This is the case of many fairy tales, in which the protagonist is usually a character that is domesticated in a competent manner and thus becomes the focus of public attention—not due to an ascendency based on a public relationship from the outset.

It is fairy-tale in nature because we like to believe that potential ascends from a domestication that is so competent, we must adhere to its substrate—even when it does not participate in public dialogue or distinction. In a way, this is the perfect sense of innocence: that potential has fled to avoid taint by reciprocation and influence, which are often seen as regulated and controlled potentials rather than natural growth.

However, even in the case of domestication that has reached competency and captured public interest, we can claim the ascendency is based on a sociality of global influence. Even if the direct lineage is a domesticated ascendancy, we can trace strands of thought and lineage to direct environmental influence.

This is not flippant, because everything is environmentally influenced at the substrate level. But even any competent domestication is often a new formation of universal aspects that transcend the natural order of domestication.

For instance, in the case of adversity, courage, and kindness, the domesticated individual may reach their own recognition of universal virtues and display such despite local sociality that does not venerate them. That veneration has reached the protagonist's heart due to an appreciation of universal aspects which have now been domesticated—but are, in fact, universal tenets that stand in opposition to the social domestication that surrounded them.

We could even go so far as to say that all competent domestication is an adherence to universal tenets against the backdrop of local sociality that displays otherwise. It is as if the domesticated individual knows of a world that deserves to be better or imagines it in a future tense—and goes against the rumination of local sociality.

That imagination, which allows for a world that does not yet exist, is based on a universal sociality that has such an ability in mind. For the localized elements, the sentiment would not be possible. But if we would follow the global movement, such a sentiment is available for its progression. For the more universal and global something is, the more available it is to its reach into the future and its possibilities.

Domestication in its natural form is a gathering of information from the most tangible universal aspects. Competent domestication, by contrast, receives the universal aspects in its most truncated and developed form—reaching even into the future for that progression.

The only way to continue in this manner is to adhere to some sort of universal system despite the prevalence of being fully contained by domestication. For it is impossible to have competent domestication while entirely playing the role of being domesticated. What would give them any advantage or perspective? It must be that the individual has seen something that the sociality around them has not.

It is the case that although it seems that the domestication which has reached competency has done so from an internal manifestation, it is rather that internal element that has seen itself in the external form and proclaimed universal tenets despite the domestication. They do not reach outside of the domestication so that they can be considered a part of that sociality, but in reality, if we follow their daily exchanges and dynamic instances, we see that they assume the role of double agent. They do so with a certain degree of class so that it doesn't appear as such and can still be proclaimed as a familiar domestication. But in reality, they are living two lives.

Because of this, we cannot say that the ascendancy was from domestication—even if the public sphere first recognized it—as being based on a local sociality. Rather, it is rooted in a universal aspect in which they have continuously lived and engaged. There would be no relatability of the public interest to a domestication that merely interacts with its most tangible aspects and its most easily readable notions, for that would just be redundant and unparticular in its nuanced aspects. It is only the case that the public will find interest in a domestication that has reached into the crevices of a universal tenet that has not been seen henceforth in regular domestication nor in universal reflection.

If we find a liminal group that appears to have a slanting in which potential ascends from their members into the public sphere, we can account for this in multiple ways. First, there is a foundational element that can consistently be proclaimed. However, it is not the *vis-à*-vis dialogue that has allowed their potential to reach its level, nor does it reflect the true nature of the work done.

The foundational element cannot be aspects such as a lineage of superior intellect, generational impetus, or a heightened sense of inadequacy that creates expectations beyond the normal social function—nor any other such factor that, while foundational, should not be considered intrinsic to the potential itself. These are mere preliminaries that have the allowance of providing direction, intention, or motivation toward the realm of potential or the ascendency of potential. It can even be the case that there may be generational trauma in which the idea of being the role of the potential in the environmental sociality is of the most significant substance.

This is not true of any direct linkage to potential in its final form, for it is merely individuals who are participating in universal tenets, having reached into that sociality to a certain sense in its proper form. We would not consider the perpetrator to have induced a trauma that has led to that potential, attributed as the ascendancy of that potential. Although a factor—like many others—they have not participated in the continuing dialogue that grants the right to proclaim any direct linkage to its sociality or ascendancy.

Another common assertion is that potential can be disputed due to the presence of surrounding individuals who have exhibited similar behavior. The issue with potential—particularly universal potential—is that it relies on a form of universal sociality, which permits any individual to access or participate in that domain. However, there will be a single individual or specific grouping that takes charge of the potential in its ascended form, and once that is assumed, there is no capacity to proclaim anything beforehand as being of that potential substance.

Furthermore, considering that not all potential—even within the same conversation—is equal, it is the specific dialogues that have developed over time between the individual and universality which have ultimately culminated in an encapsulation of potential that has accumulated to that degree. To presume that another individual has performed in the same regard is to render the entire system arbitrary. Rather, there is a great degree of nuance between individuals when ascending toward potential, even if the specific occupation is similar. We can study a particular individual to trace a lineage of thought that surpasses others in that regard, allowing us to gain insight into why they have risen above the rest.

When an individual or group takes charge of a form of potential, they retain the necessary information for the actualization of a particular sociality that cannot be replicated.

It is like a prose of poetry: there is no possibility of replicating it, for it is most nuanced in the availability of information while still retaining some coherency. In fact, there exists an entire group of individuals who retain a very high degree of potential—one that surpasses the typical judgments and critical purview necessary for interaction. In such cases, they exist at odds with general sociality, for while they do contain the potential, they further that premise to a degree where it cannot be integrated into sociality in its normal setting.

There is a possibility for the individual to interact according to all external circumstances based on an internal system. Those external interactions are only the manifest material of an already needed internal function. For instance, one can interact with family members—or with those elemental aspects in their psyche that represent those very family members.

When one engages with the form of internal interaction to contrast the external moving realm, they're doing so against the sociality of that external movement. They are pursuing the positions of an earlier frame, while simultaneously ascertaining movement against that social realm. They do this because it is available to the psyche to facilitate interaction with its subparts—it just happens that there's an external manifestation of those subparts.

Upon interaction with the external realm—after an internal mitigation was made—the individual would be inaugurated to represent a movement of that conversation, even if no conversation has commenced in the external form. It is expected of individuals, especially in adulthood, to be internally developed such that an internal mitigation does occur. The final external form, then, would be the refunctioning of developed psyches' into congruence.

We could even define this as the process of maturity: interactions no longer require external manifestation but are available to bypass such through internal mitigation.

We can regularly imagine the homecoming—whether of institutions or family bodies—where they all sprouted from a home base at a certain point in time, once aligned in dynamic function, only to return later to re-engage. Not with those old dynamics, as if merely continuing the conversation from that home ground, but rather engaging in the *adult* development of each member within the internality of the psyche, which represents that earlier dynamic.

That is why it becomes a habitat of irony, spirit, and painful realization: because it would be the case that some internalities are more developed than others. It is a habitat of regret more than anything else. The homecoming environment tends to manifest regret, as it demonstrates that certain internal development has moved ahead of others, and the realization dawns that it is too late to return, nor possible to move forward at the same pace.

We might even say the whole system of homecoming is troublesome for some individuals and may not even offer a benefit—because it only creates the realization of one's development contrasted with others, in a dynamic pool which has already surpassed the possibility of return. However, in some cases, it becomes a process of refunctioning due to noted development at each individual level.

There is continuously going to be a group or individual who maintains or retains a continuation of that home base dynamic. In some sense, they haven't matured; they are reliant upon that dynamic to continue the conversation; and for or them, it is worthwhile. It provides a tread in their step—something that has lain dormant for a long time. That movement will be far more potent than internal mitigation, because the psyche had been dependent on the external environment for that waiting period. When it finally arrives, the perceptual realm (which is stronger than internal perception) will be trounced for refunctioning.

We could dictate with some authority that if there is no grouping of the homecoming that represents the home base in its earlier environment then the entire dynamic has already shifted to some external form. The vitality of that previous dynamic depends on those individuals who continue to embody it. However, if all individuals have internally developed and moved on, at some point, there must have been an external shift in which interactions and social dynamics confirmed that the original dynamic is no longer foundational.

In these cases, there would not be a requisite for a homecoming, as there is no hosting availability of that priority. Additionally, there is no interest or memorial availability between individuals of that time and place, for it was expected that all have developed henceforward. In some sense, the homecoming itself is a prerequisite for certain individuals who have not developed internally, as well as for others who have developed but remain questionable in merit based on their attachments to that homecoming environment. They are proceeding into that dynamic because they wish to examine their internal systems based on self-consciousness—to see if it can properly mirror the external environment or if it is merely a fabrication of the psyche. The reason for their hesitation in development is that it has not been externally manifested, and thus the psyche lacks perceptual evidence that any development has occurred.

However, individuals may underestimate the possibility of external manifestation that is not reliant on the return to a home base and can be accomplished in many forms. A simple social organization that represents some of these elemental factors can be enough for a dynamic foreplay of those experiences, so they are mitigated in their external function. This will naturally manifest for the psyche because it is aware that it needs perceptual information to validate its internal development. As a result, it will seek representations of that environment to provide the habitat for that dynamic experience, though it ultimately relies on the individual to sequence that development accordingly.

We could even attribute the psychological process by which one seeks out a partner resembling their mother or father as a representation of this. This is merely a method to formalize the internal development of how one has interacted with their 'mother' and 'father.' The psyche is now seeking an external dynamic that can function as a validation or perceptual process, enabling what has been internally developed to be formalized in full, consequential form.

Now, let us consider whether there is a homecoming value intended for the internally established individual who has already externally formalized these constructs. If these constructs are assumed to be externally valid, then the homecoming process should not produce any further consequential events. Admittedly, these representations may not constitute the entirety of external development, but they can be considered sufficient for the psyche's validation. Therefore, to revisit those dynamics would be redundant and unnecessary for further psychological development.

Instead, the homecoming process should be necessary for one's present development—not in accordance with prior interactions that have already been resolved. Thus, it becomes more like a research endeavor: the attributes of those prior interactions, due to their similarities of certain developments become available for conceptual understanding in relation to one's current state.

Once prior family dynamics are re-contextualized as investigation into specific attributes of the individual's current psychological state, the focus shifts—from further dynamic development to the understanding of nuances that may have been previously missed or are only now accessible. Even if one has restored and developed from all prior interactions, they still may not have attained a nuanced understanding of the highly impactful environments that shaped their current condition.

Up to this point, we have discussed internal development in contrast to external development. Now, let us consider internal development in relation to environments, rather than sociality. There are elements of the psyche that emerge not due to specific social representations, but due to the substance of consciousness itself. These can be seen as "pockets of consciousness" that ruminate within the psyche and are channeled through narrow constructs created by interactive conflict. When one engages in mediation between these conflicting interactive elements, they gain access to the consciousness ruminating contained by each.

To explain further: once parental figures are internalized for the psyche as sources of interactive conflict, they also encapsulate latent consciousness. When one mediates these internalized figures alongside other interactive components, they gain access to the consciousness retained in that domain. Because parental figures often represent the first perceptions of consciousness—and its initial rumination—their psychological obtainability becomes immediate within the functioning of the current system.

As another example, consider two groups experiencing conflict in specific spheres of understanding. These are interactive elements not yet mediated. The idea of their conflict exists because each adheres to distinct sequences of consciousness. A group in one country is not in conflict with a distant group simply because they follow different sequences. It is not that they couldn't be in opposition, but they do not engage the same consciousness substance, and thus with no direct conflict to be experienced.

Neighboring entities that do not share a consciousness sequence will likewise not be in conflict. This explains why affluent neighborhoods often do not find themselves in direct conflict with impoverished ones—not because no perceptual conflict exists, but because they do not subscribe to the same sequence. The impoverished community may texture conflict toward the affluent due to a perceived shared consciousness substance, while the affluent do not acknowledge this shared spectrum and therefore sense no reciprocal conflict or resentment.

If communication occurs between these communities, a dynamic system can emerge—one that facilitates an agreement of consciousness. This process creates avatars within the psyche that represent components of the shared dynamic. The result is a shared consciousness that surfaces in both groups' awareness.

Ultimately, the internalization of an external experience results in a conscious disagreement. This is why communication and dynamic interaction are often resisted in these environments: the internalization of such dynamics activates conflict. One would not wish to engage in a dynamic or relationship unless they are willing to adopt the consciousness substance that such an interaction would require. This would compel an affluent individual, for example, to participate in the sequential affirmations of a broader community—potentially diminishing the consciousness sequence they previously maintained.

Thus, for conflict to arise, there must be an agreement on consequential consciousness. This agreement can be achieved in various ways. In our case, a conflict between interactive substances and the psyche—such as parental figures—requires mediation for resolution. This mediation also enables the obtainment of the underlying consciousness substance.

In essence, all conflict stems from a contest over access to consciousness. Rather than viewing conflict solely as a manifestation of mutual susceptibility towards consciousness, we can understand it as a struggle over the right to possess or access a particular conscious substance.

When conflict exists within the psyche—especially involving parental figures—its resolution allows access to the consciousness flow that was previously obstructed. If one is in conflict with internalized parental figures, they are congested from the underlying consciousness flow. Once mediation occurs and internal resolution is achieved, the individual is positioned to recover the conscious substance that had been held in conflict.

The potential process refers to the recognition of a sequential movement that might be considered the direction of evolution, while potential itself refers to the evolution of a particular sociality, all things considered. The difference between them is that the potential process can only identify themes of conjecture along a linear structure to which it attributes potential, while potential, in its full form, would be the entire linear structure in its forward movement.

Identifying a point of potentiality does not prove to be the logical continuation of evolution—only that there is a necessary evolution if we insulate this aspect and presume its growth. It could be the case that a noticed potential, if followed, would cause a reduction of the entire system, because that aspect was not essentially part of its forward movement.

By insulating a part of the process and identifying its potential, we act against the systemic movements that must account for all parts. We observe this when approaching natural vulnerabilities: we often assert that the potential of those vulnerabilities hasn't been realized without considering the entire system, which will repeatedly contain such vulnerabilities.

Demanding adherence to an insulated potential may lead to the breakdown of the system in order to satisfy that potential. Yet, the system itself created both the vulnerability and the possibility of amending it. When an insulated potential or vulnerability is pursued, the stimulation for its continuance is dampened, relying instead on a system that is fading due to those enlarged vulnerabilities. Reconciling both the system and its isolated potential can place them in opposition—or require a super-social strength to align them.

In the natural course of affairs, to obtain the insulated potential often comes at the expense of the system. The very act of identifying secluded potential presumes a lack of awareness of the whole process—something more likely to occur through third-party observation. An individual developing contained by a system will not notice their own sheltered potential, as they possess an embodied awareness of the process.

However, a third-party arbitration can take note of the secluded potential, which can spread to the individual and be supposed as a path of interest, as the potential is genuine, although the embodiment of the process is not.

The reason that a third-party arbitration can make an assumption of potential that does not include the system is because they have not endured the sociality or the parts of the system in their entirety. They are asserting claims about a system they do not inherently know, assuming an encapsulation of potential as if it were the entire scope of possibility. Usually, one would not follow or claim an encapsulation of potential without the embodiment of the specific sociality that led to its premise—but the possibility remains.

To embody the sociality is to obtain an existential awareness of the all-encompassing system in its many dynamic inferences, so as to be able to make a wholesome conjecture. This does not need to completely hold true, for otherwise one would not be able to assume any higher potential—not of others, for it is not embodied, and not of themselves, for the embodied parts are already bygone and are mere skeletal memories that do not contain the existential awareness in real-time. Yet, embodiment is the attempt to participate in the experience of each consequential event, shifting that composite picture. That picture is formed through the dynamic shifts one endures, which reflect the experience of that sociality.

For example, a classic case of potential claims is that made by the masses about the affluent. They may style conjectures about the use of the affluent' resources and treatment of social class. While there is merit to all potential, these are only processes of potential and are by no means are a derivative of the evolution of potential for the affluent. Instead, to gain existential awareness of affluence, one can follow the dynamic inferences that mirror the cases of affluence, since everyone has endured a shorter form of that process. Whether it is prominence, abundance, or any other attribute, one can follow their private dynamics and find such in a scalable format. By enduring such dynamic shifts, one can experience the comprehensiveness of what it would mean to be affluent. Through that reflection, one can then make a conjecture about its evolutionary potential. To see how these potential processes function in real-world systems, we turn now to contextual illustrations of potential in practice.

POTENTIAL IN CONTEXT (INDIVIDUAL AND COLLECTIVE)

We must understand the difference between the process of potential and potential itself, which lies in the inclusion of the sociality that led to the conjecture. The process of potential does not include the entire spectrum of sociality but instead presents itself as if it were already enjoined in that process and has now made a conclusion. This is a sleight of hand because the sociality of the process was not included, and instead, the basis of conjecture was made without allowing the material to manifest.

The material of potential is based on a social parameter in which what's included forms the premise of that potential. Therefore, we need both the sociality and its given parameters that define the process in the direction of its potential ground. For example, we need to clarify the parameters of the social system that defines affluence, in addition to including the dynamic process within that system that enables the attainability of affluence.

We can consider the meager individual and their potential within the parameters of the social system that includes the notion of meagerness, along with the dynamic process that leads one into a state of meagerness. We could ascertain *human* potential, but we are required to define *human* within the limitations of a social system and its dynamic process of engagement. Consequently, human potential is often redefined as maturity vs. immaturity, or adulthood vs. childhood.

The potential of a location is defined by its parameters and social occurrences, as well as by the dynamic engagements within that locale. For example, when we speak of "the potential of a state or country," we refer to parameters set by the entire social system, which include its internal positioning and the major dynamic shifts of the State endured during a given period. This encompasses the state's existential awareness—its understanding of its evolution—requiring a clear delineation of what is included or excluded from that potential.

We might then say that the potential of a particular State lies in expanding its economy and diversifying its investments. This assertion is grounded in the internal developments which have accumulated over time. A distinct understanding of those shifts can lead us to conclude that the State's next evolution, all things considered, should involve expansion investment and diversification. However, this claim is rather general and could apply broadly, as diversity is often assumed to be a positive developmental trait. Hitherto, there's also the risk of excessive diversification, which might prompt a need for redefinition.

In such dynamics, a child might highlight a genuine form of potential by noticing gaps in interaction and drawing attention to them. But this is only a fragment of the broader process of potential. A parent who doesn't respond to this prompting may be navigating other important processes and therefore be unavailable for such dynamic shifts. Were they to focus solely on this insulated claim of potential, they might lose sight of more substantial objectives. We observe this in individuals who over-prioritize flawless social interaction, often at the expense of larger objectives—they become caught in a loop of social responsiveness.

Still, the *annoying child* may be highlighting that the state's potential lies in a redefinition. We might imagine that when definitions fail to incorporate their historical lineage, the result is a gradual demotion or even total decline—not from malice or disorder, but from the erosion of foundational coherence.

This is how we recognize actual potential: by including all its sociality and acknowledging that, if it were missed, decline would follow. This cannot be said about the affluent in general—that they must utilize their lot for a certain agenda or objective—because their failure to do so will not necessarily lead to their diminishment. Though, if they ignore the sociality of their affluence, then they are at risk of diminishment, and in this case, we can claim their potential is led by that awareness. These claims are quite different: the sociality that has carried one to affluence is not the same as fulfilling an altruistic objective. The difference lies in their subjective inclusion in those dynamic spheres, which even altruistic objectives may not reach.

If they were once meager, this would need to be included in the sociality of their current status—but it doesn't automatically translate into an obligation toward altruism. One can gain social awareness in many forms—some connected to their affluence and others not—so the common claimant may not have made a true case for potential, but rather a fragment of their potential, which, having dealt in the manner they are seeking, may not prove to even deal with that particular claim.

The *annoying child* is another case of this phenomenon because, in some respect, the child is a catalyst to a process of potential that is true in its insulated form. That is, the child notices an unavailability between dynamic states or members and will prop with ease to downgrade their functionality and craft notice that this functionality exists in the members. This is not necessarily the complete picture of potential, but rather one sequence of events that partakes in potential.

The individual that does not perform perfectly under the guise of annoyance may, in fact, be enduring many other processes. As a result, they are not fully available for dynamic shifts. If they were to follow the secluded claim of potential, they would necessarily lose the greater substance of their objectives by focusing solely on perfecting dynamic shifts. We often observe that those who become fully engrossed in the perfection of social interactions lose sight of their objectives, as they are usually preoccupied with the circumstantial demands of social shifts and perceptual intrusions.

The annoying child may, in fact, reveal a true form of potential, having embodied the experiences of those around them. By following others' narratives and adapting to dynamic shifts, they may realize they are not functioning in full availability to the external world—specifically, in being available for dynamic shifts. Thus, they may represent the treatment or expression of the complete picture of potential.

We could argue that if we reduce the emphasis on proclaiming potential and observe a decline—meaning, if things continue in a way where dynamic shifts remain unavailable—then the prior prodding of that potential was genuine. However, if the opposite proves true—if development continues even without adherence to that claim—then we might conclude that the potential is more secluded, merely mirroring the real thing.

SOCIALITY, DETACHMENT, AND STRUCTURAL DRIFT

AN INDIVIDUAL'S OWN POTENTIAL is also a questionable realm, for it could be the case that they are pursuing an encapsulation of potential arena that is secluded from the sociality of their system. This is to say that they may lack awareness of meagre embodied states previously endured—states that have led them to this crevice of potential. Because of such lack of sociality accompanying the potential, it ascends toward an arena disconnected from its predecessors.

Yet, we can also claim that major historical figures have reached into a realm of potential that surpasses their sociality. Socrates, for example, could not have his family surround him at his time of demise; he was inaccessible to the sociality that culminated in his finale, nonetheless, reaching an encapsulation of potential that remains unequaled.[4] The possibility for such achievement lies in the notion that an encapsulation of potential secluded from embodied states can follow substrates already obtained and continue in skeletal format. In some sense, this is the process of aging itself— where potential detaches from the embodiment of sociality that originally generated it and thus becomes feebler and more formalized.

---

[4] Plato, *Phaedo*, 59e–60b.

Although this is a normal process, the complete composite of potential must include the sociality from which it emerges. When it does not, we may consider it a secluded potential, much like Socrates at the end of his life—more a persistent naysayer than one empathetically understood for their own growth or the growth of those around him.

Though, we must also recognize that to reach a state of potential typically requires the inclusion of sociality for a sustained period before detachment and loss should occur. If one detaches from sociality from the very beginning, there is no possibility of attaining an encapsulation of potential that is unmatched or unprecedented. Much like the affluent individual who, upon reaching the peak of affluence, demotes and dismisses the associated sociality that enabled that ascent—there is no scenario in which they reach affluence without that initial attachment.

Socrates serves again as an example, for he integrated sociality into his intellectual development so thoroughly that we clearly see it as a foundation for his potential. Only later did he detach—an inevitable narrowing, the mark of aging.

On the other end of the spectrum are cases where individuals prioritize inclusion of sociality in their development of potential, only for it to be detached at a certain point.

Another side of the spectrum includes cases of inclusion of sociality but at the expense of reaching potential. In the agreement and commitment to social development, one is unable to retain the imagery and the process of potential because of the anchor to that sociality. And maybe the case is that they could slowly rise above that sociality but barely far from it, and thus they endure an interactive culmination without reaching beyond to consider a place of consciousness for the good of society. In some sense, they stay familiar and adjacent, following the familial process in whatever direction it takes until they package that sociality without the ability of perceiving beyond it. This is similar to the infantile stage, having certainly not matured to consider a place where one endorses an internal development that does not agree with external sociality.

Because potential and sociality are based on the same foundation, we can note the circumstances in which they deviate from one another. The possibility of deviating itself, at least for potential, is only possible if one presumes that either a sociality exists that is not structurally founded, or if they believe potential to be an item of its own regard.

To be structurally founded is to retain a sociality that is dynamically expressed and of a certain objective form. For instance, imaginative realms of sociality—even as there is a world creation with its parameters constructed—because this is not a sociality that manifests in a political manner, it remains structurally detached.

Another example of a sociality that is not structurally founded is when the inner grouping of sociality does not adhere to its larger infrastructure, so that it acts as a state within a state. Whatever the primacy of that sociality, its inherent potential will not be structurally sound because of the disparity of its system within the larger system. This is why it is fairly consistent to ascertain political potential as being a structurally founded entity. Since it is one of the principal systems, it would automatically retain a sociality that cannot be set in stone for smaller networks. There is usually going to be disparity between structural foundations because we would not know or understand the proper encapsulation of sociality.

For potential to believe itself as a standalone system, it must retain a strong degree of repression toward the foundation of that potential. Since we acknowledge the structural inherency to potential and sociality, a presumption of their separation can only be caused by a belief that potential is something that manifests from existential matter. This would require a substantial reliance upon metamaterial theories to gain traction, for the need to justify the demotion of the background of potential must be met by a system that undergoes that which we cannot understand.

The regular notion of sociality as the provision of such potential is constantly attempting to make itself known, so a theory of reality must demote that premise time in time again. However, because metaphysical theories are developments of universal themes, it is usually the case that they will not disrupt the notion of potential for being an adversary to the genuine social system, as such theories are really an abridgment and obtainment of that very social system. This is only made possible by decrepit metaphysical theories—ones which do not retain their stature through generations and cultures—or by an extreme take on a traditional metaphysical theory that goes to great lengths to avoid any interaction with ruminating sociality and thus becomes adversarial.

However, including sociality as the mainstay for all potential will be at the expense of its potential. The most uniformed sociality is fairly bureaucratic and non-consequential regarding sentimental movement, although it arises at the behest of a great sociality.

The exchanges in the acute social setting are even going to appear redundant, as they do not include any foresight other than its direct interaction itself. This would result in all the constituents of an acute sociality to be suitable interactions which manifest as the base layer, without any egregious formats that would provide foresight or background to the interaction. This is comparable to the sociality of an early stage in a family body, in which it is common to have a sociality based on precise interactions instead of a ruminating development of theory and ingenuity.

We find that the sociality that retains a sensibility of being suspended above the interaction—so that there is a constant forward-looking movement—can be approached as a system of sociality that does not retain its bureaucratic sense and would not be considered an acute sociality. To become acute is to say that the interactions are treated at face value for the informational material within them, as if that is the actualized sentiment without any ability to see beyond or before it.

Certainly, this form of sociality is a necessity for society, because at some point we requisite a sociality that obtains and retains fair movement in real-time—one which does not have the underworkings of potential exhausting the interactions—wherever it may seem to go.

There's invariably going to be an encapsulation of potential within a social system, but because the sociality and interactions are fairly strict to those parameters, the potential is almost inconsequential. Rather, the movement itself is the primary significance of that sociality. It's almost as if there's a negotiation for still the most insignificant aspects of that structure—as well for being the systems ready to negotiate at a tapered focus, because without that, the interactions at that particular level are lost.

In a highly potentially formed social system, there is going to be a backlog of necessary interactions based on a considerable number of significant movements that have not been able to be engaged, for the weight of potential does not allow for settlement and engagement.

In every system of potential, it is necessary to retain the forward addendum and oversight, because that is the basis of potential—it does not see what is, but what could be from what is. However, in some sense, that is not the reality of the interactions or the true format of sociality, for that is only an insight into sociality in an imaginative perspective, and very often it is the case that imagination does not coexist with how reality pans out.

We cannot predict reality itself, but only what the directive of that reality is, so that we can gain a statistical analysis of where reality needs to go or where it is possible to go—but even those two elements are adversaries. Where reality needs to go is repeatedly going to be contrary to what is possible for reality, just as what is possible for reality is not going to come to an understanding with the needs of reality.

Therefore, the potential of a sociality is highly dependent on the predictability of the imaginative inference that would parallel the movement of sociality, and in some sense, highly potential systems are not genuine organizations of sociality. The most genuine of organizations are those that have the most acute interactions, because they are solely based on an interactive formula that has yet to be negotiated as a part of the social system.

However, we could also say that they are working on an imaginative problem—that of history—because they engineer that interaction at a pace that may be behind a decade or two, so that the interactions are not based on the average experience of sociality in that society. We could study the sociality of the current society and notice the necessity for those engagements which might be a decade behind, but they will not be the normalized dialogue in that system due to the latency of that information. It is almost the case that the structure itself is not interested in engaging with what has already been implemented and is fundamental to its system.

For illustration, it is not a common sociality for a society of upstanding stature to engage in discourse regarding housing-related activity. This is not because it's not a necessary interaction to developing that realm of individual life, but because there is already a bottomless history—both in personal development and in historical development—in which those interactions have already been implemented into the system. They are already considered structure itself rather than more than that. We could regularly discuss structure itself and what has already been implemented, but that would be engaging in what has already been engaged, so that it becomes a redundant talking point. There are still elements of interaction in that realm that require negotiation, and we might find that one who works in the industry will recognize that necessity. Otherwise, what has already been obtained is the implementation with a certain form of sociality, so that anything that is engaged will just be considered a lower form of interaction: bureaucratic and inconsequential to the current social system.

For example, in a bureaucratic system, there's a tendency to follow at a slower pace than regular corporeal structures; those organizations that represent the majority of potential forms of society. We could even say that they retain an interlude of a decade or two, despite the contemporary development and continuity of potential attainment.

We have not seen any change of pace in that process, despite the prevailing data of that potential, because the interactions themselves are required to take the time they need to perform at a lower level of function, all without the hovering of potentiality to lead them along. If we were to disrupt or dismember organizations that have acute sociality, we would find that the potential-oriented organizations would become more overextended by virtue of the fact that nobody in the social system is covering the lower-level interactions.

Without any development or interactivity at those lower-level interactions, they become lost to the system and labor as if they're not a part of it, so that the sociality upon which any potential system is reliant is stretched away from the interactions that prerequisite to be included in the system. This is why you will find a constant dynamic exchange between acute social institutions or organizations and the potentially formed organizations—because they are reliant on the other for provision that they cannot provide. Without the bureaucratic aspects or the acute sociality, they become lost to its innate weight.

POTENTIAL AND ACTUALITY

THE TRANSFER OF DETAILS, biological code, material property and any form that is able to be transferred, proceeds through a process which discounts the periphery and applies attention to the tangible aspects of it. We may assume that a transfer will affect the transition of the entire entity without forfeiture of any of its detailed aspects, however, being that the nature of a transfer is to be entering a new environment; one which does not contain the capacity to receive the entirety of the entity, a retrenchment must occur.

The receptive environment has a different structure. As a result, it cannot fully support the incoming transfer-material in preserving its original form. Because it is receptive, it must compromise its own intrinsic nature in order to accommodate any attainment.

There is a negotiation between the receptive environment and the incoming entity as to the amount of effacing to each of their non-vital layers so that each will progress as they become an amelioration of a final singularity. The vital elements will be considered encapsulated of the effaced aspects, which will comprise the code of the entire structure if unpacked with due scrutiny. In this manner, we can perceive that both sides of the equation are not wasting parts of their intrinsic nature, because there is a vital encapsulation that theoretically contains that information—although not readily accessible.

The possibility of decline arises when the untapped material of the encapsulated, termed as potential, may remain in its embryonic stage for an indefinite period. The path toward releasing the potential is through a conscious deliberation of its contents. This is a third-party conscious entity, which will reveal—and more importantly, make relevant—the material. We could imagine a computerized system revealing potential in this manner, but it would not be able to resolve relevancy for the biological formulation of the conscious holders, namely communal consciousness.

For instance, we can process the information of certain nuances to predict a very descriptive outcome through complex deliberation using computing models. We must agree that to revive an encapsulation of information to predict an outcome would be a form of actualizing potential. However, it is the receptivity of that outcome that will define the absolute actualization. When the consequence material is not acknowledged, or is only acknowledged for a very specific purpose, then it will not be distributed according to the relevancy of the bearer of the information.

The encapsulation of information continuously belongs to an owner. For that owner, actualization should involve the personal experience of receiving the new information. If the encapsulation is extracted and actualized into an outcome that excludes the owner's full presence, then the result is merely a representation of personhood. That outcome reflects back onto our choices. These choices appear to follow the owner's intent, but in truth, they serve us—forming a platform for our own self-consciousness to navigate potential. This process, in turn, drives the decisions we eventually make.

Although there could be a connection back to the owner of the encapsulated, if it is not deemed a worthwhile choice based on the reflection that procured upon themselves, then it will not be relevant to them. The choice was made according to their representation of an outcome, but when the eventual reception of that choice is not a fairly relevant antidote, it would not be absolute actualization.

The same can be said for any spectator, who can consistently utilize another's potential for their own actualization, but will invariably do so as a representation rather than actualization. We can follow the chain of reaction in their psyche to their own potential, which is being highlighted by their perception, to then find its peculiar actualization.

Actualizing one's own potential is usually accessed through a representation from the external realm, which guides and retains the material necessary for the process. This may undermine the development of personhood, in which a representation of potential has found pathways of actualization, demanding that one follow suit.

One can question the potential being activated to identify whether it is a limited edition of personhood or a larger portion of their depth. When the potential is limited, it is an encapsulation of information that, in its actualization, does not expand very far. We can even wonder about the necessity of encapsulating the information when, in its actualization, it becomes a very similar version of itself.

Actualization should be an enlargement to a degree that it is not noticeable within its encapsulation, and should retain a mystique for further development. Underdeveloped poetry is an example of encapsulated material, which can appear to reveal its actualization from its starting point, while developed poetry retains the depth of its actualization so that, through multiple interactions, it is perceived with an innovative actualization structure.

The character of underdeveloped poetry is that it has not been compressed thoroughly and does not include enough actualized material to initiate its process. The compression is incomplete, and the material for that very compressing is not elaborate enough. This is why developed poetry will usually contain universal themes—because that is the most

The process of poetry is the reverse of everyday life, in that it identifies actualized material and compresses it back into potential. The final product is an encapsulation of potential, but the process is a persistent retrieval of the happenstance of life.

Similarly, in life, we compress material. But this happens through natural forms of containment—not as a deliberate act. We don't typically perceive an overload of information and then consciously compress it for later use. Instead, this occurs organically, such as when one enters a new relationship or environment.

Likewise, the loss of an environment or relationship activates a comparable process. The psyche, structured by spatial necessity, disposes of what it cannot retain. When loss is experienced, it initiates a compression: some material is retained for future integration, while the rest is allowed to pass.

This is mourning—a recognition of absence that also involves the psychic act of compression. Even when the mind hasn't yet fully accepted the loss, the process unfolds internally. The external loss and internal memory may not regularly align, but the psyche continues its work, anticipating recognition and preparing material for later reengagement.

Even during an environment or relationship, this process occurs in an acute manner. A dynamic shift in a relationship will cause each party to compress the role that was previously played. When an environment is left for an intermediary period and another takes its place, such compression occurs so that the return is to a "new" environment, even if it seems all the same.

Momentary lapses in the same environment are even more acutely compressed, to the point where it seems to occur seamlessly. Every change in moment or conscious movement compresses previous data for the existing process. This very sentence has already been compressed by my psyche, and when I review its contents, it seems more general than I initially experienced.

This next sentence has the same effect as the previous one. Following that past sentence, I sense a demand to extract data. This cannot be said of a current thought, which is not extracted from itself and instead flows as fluidly as dreams. The current thought is a result of extraction, so that a strand of thoughts is based on the extraction of compressed material that has been actualized.

If we attempt to think continuous thoughts without extracting compressed material, then we loop the same thoughts. Even the loop extracts in a cyclical fashion, in which the next movement in the circle is extracting from the other side of the diameter. These may seem fairly similar—perhaps even the same thought—because the avoidance of extraction necessitates the path of least resistance. To extract what is most similar to the current data is the least difficult form of actualization.

This previous sentence will be repeated without attempting extraction: extract, repeat. Repeat, extract. Some sensible data of extraction and repetition. The world at large. Something of repetition. To repeat is to be. The horizon of reflection. Mirror. Selfhood. The awkward way in. Justifies itself. The struggle.

Eventually, the loop becomes too cyclical and implodes on itself until the last thought is "the struggle," denoting the paradox of existence to which all logic is motivated. The previous thought, "justifies itself," recognizes at least two parts of the equation: "itself" and a "moral order." Before that was "the awkward way in," describing uneasiness at an entrance—more elaborate.

Before this is "selfhood," denoting an exploration of identity, even if not explicitly defined. Prior to that is "mirror," the most compressed form signifying the entirety of the sentence's material. It is not lost to the generalities that followed, and yet it still does not contain the wholeness—compressed into a single word.

The mirror is the "current data" reflecting itself, appearing similar but still different—this is the path of least resistance. Preceding the mirror is the "horizon of reflection," pointing to the metrics of least resistance, which is lost in the single word "mirror," as it does not describe its ease of resistance in reflection.

Before this is "to repeat is to be," a philosophical assertion on cyclical patterns. Then "the world at large," which seems out of place unless we assume the scalable nature of the "world" as a demand to move beyond the cyclical pattern—or for the author to abandon this line of thought. It could suggest that the "world" naturally follows a cyclical pattern of least resistance, resulting in a lack of consciousness to which humans are beholden.

Previous to this is another variation of "extract and repeat," a justified, abridged version of the earlier sentence. Had I at any moment chosen to extract compressed data for continued thinking, this would have formed a continuous segment. The broken sentences show a lack of complete coherence.

We also see the process of compression repeating the path of least resistance, until at a certain point, it compresses with precision: that is the "mirror." After that, it becomes too general to extract data and reconstruct the original coherent sentence. Too much compression causes a loss of material, while too diminutive results in an abridged version with excessive material at the end.

If one follows this process, waiting for the best point in the downward cycle—though that point is unknown to personhood. An instance of this approach appears in the previous sentence, where I followed the pattern by invoking a string of ideas—'unknown criteria,' 'demonstrating suffering,' 'love and loss,' 'counting cards.'

The perfected compression would be in the middle two, as a downward cycle permits pain and suffering to a point. The mention of love suggests the balance needed in that process. The first thought, "unknown criteria," is too ambiguous. The last, "counting cards," simply catalogs components of the downward spiral without capturing the essence of experiencing it.

This does not mean we should now begin a discussion on demonstrating suffering, as that would be off-topic. For my psyche, the hold upon that sentence will be compressed in reference to "demonstrating suffering." Even though this introduces a new topic—emotional regulation and expression, which is more relevant to personhood—it will still be compressed in that direction.

Compression does not concern only the material itself but also its relevance to personhood. If we compress objective material down to its most perfected form, it still may not connect to personhood any more than any point of the enlarged, uncompressed data. Therefore, compression also follows the most relevant components of the material, linking them in a way that connects to personhood. It will even find external translation, making the material more retainable.

This is why, upon the loss of an environment or relationship, one reflects on components of personhood—even when that environment or relationship was not consciously tied to such complexities of the psyche.

The process towards this conscious company is through its own reflection as a piece of nature, which then proceeds with a conscious projection upon the dormant potential. The progress of this consciousness is the usage of other consciousness that has been modeled and fused onto itself.

The ability to discharge potential is relative to understanding the nature of its contents before the process of enlightening is undertaken. This seems paradoxical or unnecessary, as the one who can reveal contents must already be in association with them before the process begins. Indeed, the theoretical contents are already envisioned; however, the actuality of the contents is unknown to the individual. In some sense, the process must involve an imaginative realm, which eventually succeeds with such regard that it can then begin to enter into the actuality realm and reveal its contents.

This conceptual transformation echoes through myth and psychology, especially in the framework of the hero's journey. In such a narrative, the individual must rehearse the future in an imaginative space before it can be realized—focused instead on shaping a possible or ideal future which eventually must be attended. Rather, it pertains to a sort of fantastical realm that grants them a sense of awareness of their future endeavors.

This practice remains with some sense of what the future holds, but without the realistic experience of such. Even as there is no truth to that preparation, the mental arena prepares itself—even as it agrees it's imaginary—so that the hero can reveal the final potential with the knowledge of its already-known contents. We may ask if one can accomplish through the imaginative realm, and it would not be necessary to enter the realistic realm for something quite similar.

This can be understood by recognizing that the imaginative realm only gives knowledge of the actual potential that must be understood prior to the enlightening process. While there is no special attention to be had for the final situation, the practice has been so meticulous. The knowledge that has been attained in the practice is necessary to enter into the potential itself, which is only deserving of special attention because it meets at the realistic juncture of life.

There is a failure in expounding the imaginative realm further than required, and by not giving adequate attention to its realistic manifestation. Because human relations are the epitome of manifestation, when the imaginative realm is not realized in human interaction, it becomes corrupted with the assumption of non-humanistic particulars.

For instance, the hero's preparatory journey may be overstimulated with an oversight of sensitive material pertaining to the defeat of their adversary. The oversight is caused by lingering in the imaginative realm for too long, thus having the individual deviate from the general picture with a single-mindedness on an assumed aspect. When the moment to intersect the imagination with reality fails, the ensuing moments involve an assumed adversary different from the realistic one.

Soon, the entire situation is far removed from reality, and all further preparation only deviates more from the intended results. However, being that one can stumble upon any form of success in the imaginative realm, the deviation can prove effective in dealing with another aspect of reality—quite different, but fulfilling to a realistic manifestation. The only difference is that the imaginative landscape is built upon an individual who had no interest in that sociality until they fell upon that moment of triumph.

Thus, the final manifestation arises through self-denial at the individual level of expansion, as if they had intended such an objective all along. This places them in a moment of realistic manifestation which is not paralleled with personhood. That original journey had failed, and the secondary moment of unintended manifestation is assumed to be primary. There would be no way to move forward if this process of self-denial did not take effect, as there would be no availability to betray personhood—even if there is a possible realistic manifestation. To accept that it did not ascend from personhood but by accident does not allow for continued attention, as this would betray personhood. Even as the happenstance has them stumble upon a possible realistic manifestation—which gives a certain right to follow despite the intended objective—the betrayal of personhood remains the same.

Although there will be little surprise at its information, the actuality of it will allow for the finite of the details and its interaction with one's existential self. For in the instance that one is only regulating in the imaginative realm, it will not be actualized with the entirety of selfhood. Personhood will contain a strand which does not interact with the content, and this will effectuate an eventual deviation even as the imaginative realm has seen success. The deviation will be caused by its lack of integration with reality, which will leave a part of personhood detached from the details and consequently discontent with the process. The partial aspect of selfhood will act against and in protest to a realistic set of affairs, and this will be part of the cause of deviation.

Another point for that effect is the dismissed details, which can only be seen in the case of actuality. These details will seem inconsequential to the imaginative realm but will be such when experienced in actuality. Therefore, the process of the imaginative realm which then enters the realm of actuality is the natural progress of growth. When the realm of actuality is brought to its final contentment, another process of an imaginative realm can secure a procedure which will begin the case of theory upon all that has been actualized.

To reveal potential would require a preconceived layer of what it already contains, which will then be applied in actuality. Yet, through the contained actuality, we can begin a process of questions to another imaginative realm which attempts at a layer that discounts the agreed elements of that actuality. This is the process of critique, which attempts to undermine aspects of that actuality so that another imaginative realm can be built. The critique cannot undermine the entire structure, for then there is no lineage to the next realm of actuality. There should be a fundamental base which retains its skeletal structure so that the imaginative realm contains an actuality-base for its vitality.

We can imagine that, without a material realm, the imaginative realm is only given free rein to the extent that the material realm can reproduce it. When the imaginative realm operates without anchoring itself to the realm of actuality, it becomes detached from conscious vitality and ultimately fails to sustain the complexity it inherently requires.

This becomes the process of reproduction—to which the production-to-reproduction link has been neglected—so that it becomes an attempt at progress that contains a weaker propagation forum. When this neglect goes on for too long, the recurrent cycle of reproduction becomes a model of the production, which is projected as if it were reproducing. The model itself will begin to be the entirety of the forward progress, so that the father, in neglect of his existential reality linked with *his* father, will project *his* father to vitalize the reproduction without the slightest change of reproduction. This can cause a lineage of generations to be existentially similar, for each point is projecting their father for future reproduction.

As in the process of critique, when undermining the entirety of the entity under review, it will reconstruct an imaginative picture that is the same as the entity under critique. Although it would seem to be a progressed model, we can identify the existential structure to be the same—with a change of color or terminology. This can be problematic when there is due reason to question a reality structure, yet because it is done with such veracity devoid of protecting the fundamental layer, the process of growth becomes a projected model of the exact aspect under critique.

The imaginative realm begins gaining traction when there is a completion of the actuality realm. The completion is not enjoyed with contentment, because upon its relaxation, one finds their existential state to be empty. For we do not contain the answer to our existence, and it is a tangible, fleeting entity. The completion of something will be the start of the imaginative realm.

We cannot progress within the realm of actuality because it is grounded in material exchange. For example, if we want to advance the condition of a homebody, we must conceptually step outside that domain and enter an imaginative realm of intellectual data, which can then be reapplied to the material context. Progress made solely within the homebody's domain will be limited by a blindness to the domain's totality. As a result, certain specific points of interest may be mistakenly highlighted as indicators of progress, even though they may actually distract from a more meaningful or true advancement.

Within the structure, we will only see what is in front of us, while outside the structure, with an imaginative layer, we will see above and through it. We understand that a general point of view does not account for the actuality realm, and this is mediated when there is an integration, as we discussed. However, the perspective of the imaginative realm accounts for the scope and breadth of the entirety of the picture. The limitations of the actuality realm are very restrictive to the singular experience of the moment. The imaginative realm removes the subjective midpoint and allows for a scope of availability.

There are still restrictions, as the imaginative realm is being supported by the actuality realm and will generate a perspective that is related to it. Still, there is a subjective midpoint within the imaginative realm, who may be considered an avatar assumed to be in the experience of the imagination. We need these avatars to replicate the subjective midpoint, as we cannot remove the normative structure of reality even within the imaginative realm.

When the actuality realm is sustained without being receptive to the calling for an imaginative realm, it becomes a habitat of confusion and lacks complexity. Even as it derives constant energy—because it is the realm of actuality and thus available to the conscious distribution—it becomes an encapsulation which goes deeper into itself and becomes sheltered from the capacity for it to be unpacked. It awaits in darkness, falling into itself. Yet at a moment's notice, a conscious individual can enter its domain and extract its data, as if it had never been under shelter. Although the holder of that encapsulation will be lost into the background once the extraction is complete, they had only been a successive individual because of the contents within that encapsulation, just like this new individual.

The imaginative realm can also be actualized while still maintaining its substructure as a form of imagination. The actualization is to experience the materiality of the imagination while still detracting from a full integration. The motivation for such a pathway is to define the details of the imagination at the furthest point so that, with the final integration to complete actualization, it will be a promised success.

There is a problem with an imaginative realm which does not allow preceding actualizations to follow its theory, as the disparity will be great. Upon full integration, this will be costly to both theory and the previous reality structure. However, the makeshift arena which actualizes the imaginative realm without any real integration is performative materiality, no different than a theater performance. The structure is a façade and is only interacted so as to define the imaginative realm and perform the integration with actuality. We cannot dismiss such activity as superfluous because we require the experience of the imaginative realm in its details before we begin the integration process.

Firstly, this makeshift arena will highlight the existent reality structure in its detail, which will enable a transparent picture of the state of affairs. Secondly, it will provide the experience of the imaginative realm alongside existential aspects of personhood, thus granting a preliminary foresight into the imaginative realm with its eventual actualization.

We cannot visit the state of reality from a point of view according to its actualization because the experience is adjacent to the individual, and cannot perceive its details from an external vantage point. As well, we cannot imagine the actualization of the imaginary realm without a form of actualization.

The makeshift area will become problematic when it is viewed as the actualization—post-integration, for which it is a sense of completion. There is no sentiment of advancing toward another imaginary layer, as in the real scenario of completion, so that a sense of existential contentment takes effect. For in some sense, all realms are completed—the imaginary, for there is a makeshift actualization; and the actualization, for its completeness.

Thus, a point of stagnation arises, for which there is conscious vitality that leaks from the state of reality as it is; although erroneously perceived as the imaginary realm which has been actualized. The sense of intimacy experienced will be attributed to the imaginary realm which they have been entertaining. All the while, it is the imaginary realm which disrupts the intimate experience that seeps in from the previous actualization of reality—almost as if there would be no need for the imaginary realm to be sought.

Its only utilization is to halt the existential sense that has one progress from the state of actualization towards a new imaginary layer. It provides an existential cushion for the purpose of providing continuous intimacy from the previous state of actualization, which is not recognized as the source of all of their experience.

Part IV – Actualizing Personhood

CHILDHOOD ACTUALIZATION

ACTUALIZING REALITY is another term for the experience of taking what is internal and allowing it to manifest into a broader nest of actualization. In every situation, it can be viewed as a seed waiting for a womb to actualize itself. Although, when we view such an aspect at a human level, we assume that the final process was enacted through birth, one can still perceive this process recurring, with further actualization processes available for actualization.

For instance, a young child who matures into a young adult has actualized a further context, making them a more realized entity in its broader terms. These broader terms make the human being more than they were, and as such, to judicially process their actions and intentions accordingly.

The actualization of a child is different from that of adults and can parallel to that of an indigenous individual who first partakes in advanced civilization. This should not be confused with later actualizations, which require much more nuance and a complex degree of integration.

Because a child does not yet possess the imagery or fantasization that informs how actualization takes effect— since they do not, at large, have the acquisition of civilized nuance—their early, meager actualizations of any sort will not be costly to their persona. For example, a child may play with dolls or trucks, actualizing, in that regard, the political sense of a budding sculptor or the trucking industry at large. Still, one would not classify the child as a trucker, sculptors, mothers or political entities, because they are not, in fact, actualizing to the extent of real-world engagement.

Although they may emulate trucking or motherhood, or embody the spirit of the doll in play, they lack the full knowledge and experience in the intricate details of these roles. Therefore, the actualization only takes effect according to their level of expertise and development. Many children will play with trucks and dolls but, in adulthood, will usually not consider themselves to be part of those industries or trades. Instead, they are merely actualizing in an alignment with their understanding as children. Their play reflects only the necessary aspects of the truck or doll relevant to their stage of domestication.

Their level of expertise is applied with a kind of political relevance: the truck "works," and all is emulated in parallel and sequence—but only to the extent of their current understanding. There is a subliminal understanding that never departs, so that the adult also takes perspective on the sculptured item or its political manifestations, but applied at a fair level of understanding, so that the political relevance doesn't go away, but its application is a varying consequence.

For example, the average adult may perceive a truck as an infrastructure item—an emblem of society—and interpret it accordingly. The child, on the other hand, may see that same truck as a father figure, a mother figure, or a representation of the familial home body. That is their frame of reference, and so their actualization follows according to it. It leaves less of a dramatic effect because their actualization does not carry an overwhelming presupposition about the nature of reality.

For adults, each actualization becomes increasingly dramatic, as it functions within a broader sequence of reality. Their actualizations run parallel to their level of understanding. Since their understanding is complex and deeply tied to reality as a whole, every act of actualization contributes to shaping both their perception and their reality itself.

PREREQUISITES: BIOLOGICAL ACTUALIZATION

THERE ARE PREDOMINANT prerequisites to enabling biological actualization. The first is biological necessity, and the second is biological relation. Biological relation is simply the connection between biological habits and a current endeavor. Biological necessity is the requirement for fulfilling the biological system—without it, fissures and disruptions would occur.

Without biological necessity at a fundamental level, the system would lose the capacity to actualize. Without biological relation, it would also lose actualization because it would lack the required connection.

However, there is a third category: attention to the attenuation of the circumstance. This is not a formal prerequisite—actualization will occur with or without attenuation—but attenuation determines how strongly the actualization influences the psyche.

We are reminded that actualization is only the first step; once one is delivered from psychic retrenchment, one participates in that actualization. We could draw actualization from the environment, but it becomes a truly salient endeavor only when the foundation of actualization is already laid and ready to receive it. For instance, we could shape a child to adopt adult mannerisms or to participate competently in adult structures, but we would not have gained much ground— because the child's psyche has not reached a level where those mannerisms add real depth. The actualization merely overlays the existing system without fundamentally enlarging it.

As previously noted, consciousness is, at its root, a reflection; actualization is simply the realization of that reflective process. The construction of a psyche—using our example, for a child to become an adult—requires a new set of parameters. But it is safe to assume that it is based on the construction of the psyche that the actualization has its effect.

This is where things become delicate. As noted, attenuation and psychic contraction govern the degree and reception of that actualization. An incompetent psychic construction can produce a strong attenuation, thus gaining entrance to a nuanced actualization that does not fundamentally enlarge the system—because the contraction was not completed. In this case, one is actualizing beyond one's means and is able to do so only through attenuation.

This is the nature of many chronological mystical figures: they communed with actualization despite their contraction, using attenuation to access a vast reservoir of information— yet being unable to obtain, retain, or apply it practically. They become vessels of actualization without ever being fully actualized. This is why one must be wary of attenuation: it grants access to an actualization that is not foundational to the psyche's construction.

Without attenuation, one would actualize only in accordance with one's psychic construction. However, once attenuation is introduced, systems fail to retain actualization beyond their built capacity. The environment then actualizes a psyche that cannot sustain it, degrading both psyche and environment.

Even without attenuation, biological necessity plus biological relation can drive actualization beyond a psyche's development. For instance, a child repeatedly immersed in over-competent environments—given necessity and relation—would actualize beyond means. This reinforces the notion that they may exhibit adult-like stature despite having an infantile psychic construction.

This can lead to an addictive cycle: repeatedly actualizing an under-developed construction only to reenact the same limitations. It then appears impossible to depart from this state and reach a more developed reality; instead, the individual keeps striving to attain the actualization that would prevent them from facing their reality. These prerequisites set the stage for the next step: understanding how actualization unfolds through structured internal and external processes.

ACTUALIZATION: PROCESS AND REPRESENTATION

ALTHOUGH THERE is a concept of structural environments and the actualization of each in accordance with their level of consciousness depth, there is a psychological process that precedes them. Hopefully, our inquiry will lead to a convergence between the psychological happenstance and the structural reality.

As we have noted, there are two primary components to decipher a structural environment, and two secondary components. The two primary ones serve opposite extremes: the first being the central locale, which is for the purpose of actualization and is the leadership of the consciousness substance that becomes necessary for all other components; the second is the interactive realm, as this is the locale that allows for the validation and interaction of specific parts of its system without involving the wholesome nature of the system—in other terms, the wholesome endeavor versus its differentiation.

Regarding the psychological happenstance, however, this is not enough of an interpretation, because we have dictated that any actualization in the department of the central locale will be the direction of all differentiation, so that any wholesome interpretation of the psyche does not have the effect of dissemination to all the differentiation possibilities. Instead, it is more of a symbiotic relation, where there is a turn to the generality and to the other, of the differentiation—each in service to the other.

Actualization is the term that is more significant here, in which the psychological system can actualize and can halt its actualization. Generality is closely associated with actualization, but they do not come from the same source. One can be general, such as the idea of all humans, but still not actualize themselves as fully embodying that idea in an existential manner, to the point that they become *that* idea. Instead, we will repeatedly find generality that comes alongside actualization, but not the opposite. Actualization is when the psyche takes the existential state and places it upon the informational happenstance.

This occurs naturally in the higher consciousness realm, as would be in the central locale, because one mirrors the environment so that they notice the degree of existential depth—so that they accept that the information outside is more developed than the current internal system. A psychological system is based on a certain actualization which, at one point or another, was recognized as more developed than the current model; it is the consciousness block that is of a great depth.

Similar to a structural environment, in which the actualization is the most directive and competent part of the environment, the individual will naturally process and flow in the direction of a higher level of confidence. With every encounter of the environment or individual, one will become a part of that consciousness.

Consciousness becomes a natural process—one synchronizes with the environment or with sociality—and there is a very complex process to halt this normal, natural direction. However, there is the matter of the psychological system, in which it does follow a set of parameters so that the consciousness is still a chosen event. One can technically actualize whatever they see fit, only by choice—that they choose to existentially attach not to what is consciousness substance, but more so to a possibility of a specific direction.

If we are to accept that one can actualize any idea, individual, or environment, then it follows that the process of actualization can be chosen—whether when the environment demands it or when it does not. To actualize something is to determine the current setting of processes in which one takes the leadership to reflect those processes upon the area of actualization so that it can incur the resemblance and thereby the direction of change. Actualization cannot occur where the regular system simply takes on new information, since if it is in the direction of regular dynamic exchange, then it is not an actualization but an addition of interactivity.

Additionally, actualization cannot occur where one dismisses the current interactivity in order to participate in a new display of experience and information, for the current system does not have the fortitude to properly engage in that realm. Therefore, actualization occurs when we take the current system and have it reflect and represent itself in the new realm so that it can lead to a certain promotion, which both interacts with the current system in addition to reaching beyond it to an entirely new realm.

The information is being used to reflect and represent, serving merely as a bridge—one that neither requires adherence to the rules of dynamic exchange nor leads to the advent of a new realm disconnected from the current one. Even if one were to dismiss current interactivity, actualization will still reach into the database of interactivity, as it requires a semblance of recognition in order to understand and participate in the new realm.

Representation serves as the bridge of actualization, and it becomes an anomaly when one chooses to actualize an event that is already in participation with their interactivity—since that event should go on to represent itself to its own informational structure. One would need to glorify this event in order to act as if it constituted a new environment, thereby allowing actualization to take effect—such that representational activity follows from their current information. This leads to the glorification of selfhood, wherein current interactivity becomes represented unto itself and revitalized by the very fact of being proposed as something greater than it is.

This creates a cyclical process. The pressed actualization effectively deems current interactivity insufficient and incites re-participation of a new system that is ultimately composed of the same substance of consciousness—so that one ends up chasing their own tail. They dismiss the competency of their internal state in order to actualize with that very same competency, thereby maintaining themselves through an act of actualization that simultaneously dismisses and revitalizes their internal structure.

This is what occurs when one attempts to actualize any interactive domain after its initial actualization. They maintain the status quo through a perpetual cycle. While this may appear relatively harmless—merely a matter of wasted time— it can prove detrimental to individuals who have already participated in a more sophisticated realm, because these repetitive actualizations disrupt the integrity of higher-level competency.

To make this more explicit, let us enter into a direct example. A distinct form of interactive material is one's childhood sentiment toward their parents. This remains interactive to the adult, but at one point, it was actualized to be interactive, with a preliminary interactive material behind it. As we do not need to be microscopic about the depths at which it reaches, we will accept the current sentiment to be the adult-containing interactive substance of details between themselves and their parents. Note that this material is not re-realized or altered in any manner, and the sentiment in childhood is retained in the exact format within adulthood, with the only exception being that there is a perimeter around that interactive material that is refined.

At this point in adulthood, this interactivity remains at the bedrock of the system and remains fixated like the sun, with the planets interrelating to it. The reason it does not change, while other surrounding interactivity can still interact and change, is that the alternative interactivity is seeking validation, to which it will variate for realignment.

In this example, when the adult encounters another person, their response is shaped in accordance with those early parental relationships. The new individual is coerced into predetermined forms that preceded them, so that the current interactivity is only in its perfection at validation to its most relatable ally in the past. The reason that this interactivity has the ability to change, while the one preceding does not, is because the recent interactivity is utilizing a certain aspect of reflection and representation from the onset. Instead of viewing the current interactivity as *unadulterated*, it is an assortment of both representing the parental sentiment and purporting its similarity as an interactive validation.

When we remove the representational effect from the current relationship, it becomes more fixated and consequently a semblance of the parental experience in a genuine format. Meaning that no longer is there an attempt at alignment, but rather it is acted as if there is a relationship between that sentiment and the current one, so that they validate each other. In this way, there is an influential change between the longstanding and current sentiment based on that dynamic. However, because the perfected validation would require one to reimagine the entire landscape of childhood experience, although the change would be forthcoming, a disruption of adulthood would incur. In effect, the child will be re-actualized.

This is why it is only natural for the adult to fuse representation and interactivity—so that the representation allows the new relationship to be actualized within current development, while interactivity provides space for subtle alteration and convergence of experiences. This complex negotiation is precisely why it takes such a lengthy and demanding process to establish a new familial body. It requires a constant oscillation between representational activity (as a form of recreation) and validation through interactivity, which carries forward early sentiment.

There is no way to accelerate this process. Direct interactivity risks reverting into childlike action without the framework to preserve adult development—resulting in a form of success that is, paradoxically, a regression. Similarly, overuse of representation without genuine interactivity reduces all relationships to environmental objects—tools of self-actualization without any potential for interactive growth. While not inherently harmful, the absence of a procedure for interactive semblance causes future actualizations to rest on infantile sentiments and their reflections. The result is a leap—from the dramatic impulses of a child to the complexity of adult life—without the proper framework of education or social integration. One outcome damages the individual; the other threatens society as a whole. The former is the erosion of individuality, and the latter the disintegration of sociality.

FRAGMENTATION OF THE PSYCHE

As we conclude this examination of personhood, we must confront its greatest threat: the fragmentation of the psyche when consciousness is compromised. The actualization had the effect of realizing the psyche in its specific components, explaining why it loses its connection to the rest of the psyche—namely, that the entire psyche relies on consciousness or its representation to grant any access to itself. Thus, we can assume that, in its unactualized form, the psyche almost does not exist—not only for itself but even within the subconscious layers.

We are proposing a revolutionary idea: that the partialization of the psyche, which does not gain access to actualization as long as we consider it a wholesome actualization, would render the rest of the psyche absent from any realization. The subconscious layers associate only with the particles that pertain to the actual psyche because actualization is the rudimentary stage of consciousness, and consciousness is what grants access to the psyche.

Therefore, we are presented with the possibility of access that only gives rise to the effects realized within that realm of access. Mental capacities that are not attached to consciousness or representation exist only in a material effect—meaning there are plasma connections related to those elements, but they lack access to consciousness. As a result, they remain fragments of organic function, much like a cell of the skin rather than a cell of the brain, which we regularly consider most significant for giving rise to conscious experience.

Part V – Capabilities of the Collective

THE COMMUNAL CHARACTER

THE COMMUNAL ENVIRONMENT is a subject worth investigating, particularly in how the relationship between the individual and the collective functions. We could refer to the collective as the 'communal character,' which represents the average person of a given setting. This individual is intentionally constructed without personal traits to symbolize the general characteristics proposed for a human being. This task is quite a feat for even a communal character, as no personal characteristics naturally enable the embodiment of a shared persona. However, we are granted the possibility of performing such an artistic feat by entering the realm of imagination, thereby offering this perceived individual certain capabilities unavailable to the typical individual.

FIRST: FREEDOM FROM PERSONAL EXISTENCE

One capability of the communal persona is its transcendence of individual identity. In this mode being free from the centrality of personal existence, as we ask it to become the embodiment of any single person. This communal character cannot experience subjective pain or pleasure because doing so would detract from its primary attachment to the commonality of humanity. When averaging multiple people, the replicated reference cannot experience personal success or failure. Analogous to statistics, which excels at creating a transparent analysis of a given situation but falls short of accounting for the nuances of distinct individuality within that representation, the communal character can only serve as a general reflection of humanity. Statistics are a reliable way to understand commonality, as they represent humanity without accounting for individual subtleties. Kant describes this characteristic as unrefined, stating that what is everywhere lacks qualities that confer distinction upon its possessor. (Kant, 1790).[5]

SECOND: PROCESSING COLLECTIVE INFORMATION

Another core trait of the communal entity is its ability to synthesize information across multiple individuals its ability to understand the collective information within a given setting. It can process this information and produce a theme of commonality. This is a sleight of hand since we are fabricating the individual and consequently granting ourselves this power. However, this analysis is incomplete, as we are not in direct exchange with every person in the community, nor can we fully synthesize a theme from that information. Nevertheless, we contend that this task can be approached through a lens of generalization, akin to any deliberate oversimplification.

THIRD: IMPARTIAL REPRESENTATION

This capability allows the communal body to act as a neutral interpreter of social input, having the communal character empowered in a way that does not make particular judgments about whatever it represents; it is not self-conscious or self-aware. If this individual understood from a specific perspective—representing common humanity—it would make self-derived decisions concerning that representation. It is a representation without the burden of consequences, failures, or defeats. It does not concern itself with where it ends

---

[5] Immanuel Kant, *Critique of Judgment*, (1790).

up or what the future holds. Its only concern is the extent to which it embodies the commonality of humanity, and the proportion of output that can be derived from this communal character.

We can view this from two perspectives: one is the objective ability of the communal character to carry essential information about the collective social experience, and the second is a subjective point of view of the individual interacting with this figure, and the level of complexity they bring to the interaction. The relationship between the two may yield differing interpretations of what constitutes the commonality of that sociality. For example, the commonality perceived in the some may center on individualism and liberty. The communal character thus represents that, in parallel with a certain consistency within the general public at the existing moment.

The way the public interacts with this theme will influence how it manifests for this communal character. However, if one interacts with more complexity, they may uncover underlying philosophies. For instance, liberty may be seen as opposing authoritarian systems, but not necessarily advocating for freedom from all systems. Manifestly, we might interpret this to mean that liberty is only about freeing oneself from domineering systems, in favor of other institutional identities.

This view can evolve as the population moves towards advocating for liberty from all forms of institutional identity. In such a scenario, the emphasis would shift toward the promotion of a strictly personal identity. Thus, someone who interacts with the communal character in this manner enters into a domain that is outside the normativity of the collective. This process resembles entering another's subconscious—a realm where individual intentions are absorbed by the communal psyche and restructured collectively and declaring it the true representation, while in normal interactions, that subconscious material is often evident.

Apart from the complexity of the person interacting, the objective assembly of the individual also adds an element of complexity. Even a person with the ability to approach the relationship with complexity may still encounter its limits if the commonality of man in a given setting is fragile or lacks a developed philosophy. For instance, as we have said, liberty can represent a constitution within this individual; yet, elsewhere in the ethical or philosophical system, liberty can be apprehended differently, such as the liberty for one to degenerate. The availability of this communal character is limited when discussing such an inquiry, representing only the commonality of man, and confined to certain philosophical structures, ideas, and beliefs. When we transcend those, we enter a domain beyond the complexity of this commonality.

FOURTH: THE PERPETUAL STATE OF HAPPINESS

The communal character performs acts of substitution, allowing individuals to symbolically offload. There is an authority to regularly persist in the realm of consciousness and awareness, never experiencing a dejected state or existential crisis. Essentially, it is regularly contented and joyous, as that is the only method of transmission when dealing with generalities. Even when that sociality is in a state of melancholy or mourning, the contrived individual will reflect these emotions in an imaginative form, without personally experiencing them. It is parallel to someone who finds excitement in recounting tragic events without truly feeling the tragedy themselves.

Since the perceived individual is merely an embodiment—an actor—it cannot transmit without a conscious connection. This means that those who partake in the connection to this communal character can only do so as a method of study within the conscious realm. When the information is not found within the consciousness realm or is rather in a state of existential chaos, the creature will be unattainable, being something conceptualized and fashioned. In such a state, we are bound to what is truly interactive and dynamic—something that engages the existential state, reciprocating in parallel with one's interaction.

The communal character, an artistic representation of statistical analysis, remains inaccessible during states of depression or existentialism. We only concern ourselves with statistics as a foremost generalization of a situation to enable progress in the realm of consciousness. We could imagine pastoral societies uninterested in interacting with statistics, as they might assert, "You are missing the point" or "It is too complex to be generalized."

That is the theme: the communal character anthropomorphizes the data with its relevant and irrelevant symbols to portray the average situation. Therefore, the commonality of man, or common sense, can only be interacted in a state of higher consciousness. As noted, melancholy cannot be accurately represented or conveyed from a position of genuine depression, as this would not align with the subjective experience. Only an entity with a sense of self and an understanding of its innate existence can truly experience melancholy.

FIFTH: THE ILLUSION OF PERFECTION

This capability sustains the illusion of flawlessness, often suppressing individual failure or doubt. Faults are bound up with individuality, which acts from a central position that can decipher right from wrong. This is not the case for the communal character, who is unable to experience themselves or assert clear judgments. This, certainly, is another self-identified authority enacted by assuming the communal character's perspective is genuine. This communal character is assumed not to miscarry and can be seen as "the communal body" in all its parts.

We can critique the communal body, but we do so by using this collective identity to relate to individuals who perform tasks that challenge our notions of existence. A state, for example, cannot commit wrongdoings in the same way an individual can; only the constituents within it can be wrongdoers. We prefer to relate to them established by their attachment to the state's identity. Criticizing a communal body is far simpler than engaging with its individual members. It is easier to target a collective system than to confront the intricacies of a single person,

Sincerely adopting the communal persona transforms into a perceived maliciousness, as one becomes a communal engine. We share the fortune of engaging with that persona, one which does not concern itself with any humanness and becomes pent up with the aforementioned characteristics. This is not "them" acting wrongly, for they, as people, are not part of the equation; only the communal sense is their experience of selfhood and the world. We find people who systematically depart from their individuality and partake with full devotion to this persona. However, the label of maliciousness is applied only to those who enact the communal representation in a manner that manifests the negative aspects of the communal body.

They are equally wrong in micromanaging communal identity, yet we find disfavor with those who do so, which casts a shadow on the face of all communal bodies. We may impede them with great judgments of wrongdoing when they have done nothing erroneous from a social standpoint. Expecting a predisposed representation of the communal body, presenting a distorted view of something terrible, might be considered more morally problematic than someone doing so sincerely. Their individuality corrupts the current stream, both representing the community with its associated respect and steering away from the unsettling reality of it.

The fate of the communal body is one of confusion, since many representatives are acting from a pathological vantage point that does not acknowledge reality. We may question why these individuals gain representative status by diverging from "common sense." The answer lies in their initial rise to distinction: at a certain stage, they accurately represented the commonality, which empowered them to depart from the mainstream. Quickly, however, that dissipates into a hypothetical realm, as the reality was grimmer than would be appreciated by the masses.

This is great irony: we critique a communal body for lacking concern for humanness, which is also the method we use in making that very critique. We are standing in a communal sense, admonishing another communal body for its lack of individuality, while we relate from a non-individualistic framework. We are condemning those who erased individuality with a method that eliminates individuality.

The ability to create illusions is a complex criterion to carry out, but it becomes a major method of influence. The entire validity of its existence depends on the perceived reality of its nature, requiring it to be highly manipulative in its interactions. It seeks to enthrall that it is more realistic than, say, one's unique perspective, or that oneself is the true fabricator of the entire system. Kant highlights this sentiment: "which in its reflective act takes account of the mode of representation of everyone else, in order, as it were, to weigh its judgment with the collective reason of mankind, and thereby avoid the illusion arising from subjective and personal conditions which could readily be taken for objective, an illusion that would exert a prejudicial influence upon its judgment."

The ability to create illusions is remarkable, as the subjective mode possesses an ability to naturally elude the watchful eye of its inherent system. This might have one consider the entire situation a fallacy of civilization that has men become pathologically pinned against themselves. However, we may not have to spend our questions expediently upending social ideas if, after all, we are the representation of nature. We can conclude the following: human cognition contains natural pathological pockets functioning as distinct organisms. Preceding religious identity, we still adhered to makeshift domains of perspectives to distribute information into our systems. Essentially, we enact smaller worlds within our world, which replicate the 'universal world' downcast to diverse levels of experience. The notion of civilization is attached to this smaller world within experience, which can then offer an illusion to the rest of our experience. The illusion is meant to be temporary, as would be the multitude entering a magic show, which would become meaningless had they not had the readiness to be amazed in contrast to strict truth.

We will debate the merits of Kant's proposed union between the communal character and us, departing from a factual relationship, understandably with its troubling characteristics, and treating it as an object to simply be incorporated with. "If he detaches himself from the subjective conditions of his judgment and reflects upon internal judgment from a universal standpoint, which he can only determine by shifting ground to the standpoint of others." (Kant, 1790)[6]

Shifting one's position may lead to the loss of individuality in favor of commonality among people. This results in a lack of a strong judgment, much like that of a defendant in a legal inquiry. Reasons arising from a shift into communal awareness may lack a central perspective, making it difficult to interpret information cohesively. We may say that the analytic mode of the mind will need to work more than what is proper to resist the temptation to appear inconsistent. Thus, rationality or reason becomes the safe haven to ensure that whatever was achieved from the communal leap is somewhat sound. However, embedded within this final form of reason, we could identify a lack of individuality, which makes the notion of reason arbitrary.

Engaging with this 'non-individualized' communal sense with a degree of relational value is more challenging than Kant proposes. This provides a sense of freedom from rigorous *reason*, enabling individuals to engage with all their principles intact. We often wonder at those who propose such strict forms

---

[6] Immanuel Kant, *Critique of Judgment*, (1790).

of reason, as if individuality is somehow exempt from participating in that interaction.

We may find the romantic notion which, as Rousseau proposed,[7] is completely absent in the wording of Kant: "the greatest of all prejudices is that of fancying nature not to be subject to rules which the understanding, in consequence of its essential laws, lays at its basis."

The entire system of judgment, reason, and the mind is assumed to be governed by the rules of nature. This discounts the entire apparatus of experience, which is dismissed if not fit into the articulated rules of nature, let alone aspects that are not subject to rules or are too subtle to attribute parameters.

Considering the troubling portrayal of this communized individual, we might contemplate its potential benefits for sociality. However, in doing so, we are also justifying the existence of the communal body itself, as it is only relevant based on this perception. Without any interaction, the communal body and its ability to represent itself essentially fades away. This communal character is the lifeline of the conceptualization of a communal body. The degree of potency that the communal body has upon individuals depends on its level of interaction. The creation of this individual is performed by individuals who seek to authenticate the communal body. Thus, there will be many prerequisites for the performance of a communal body and/or the maintenance of it.

---

[7] Jean-Jacques Rousseau, *Discourse on the Origin and Foundations of Inequality among Men*, Rousseau emphasizes the intuitive and emotional connection between humans and nature, often seen as a foundation of Romanticism.

The communal character will not take notice of with whom it is interacting and will make no attempts to further any relationship. The relationship lacks the property of *relating* back, as in a typical relationship, consequently missing vitality and relevance. It is pathologically absorbed on having the communal body under its invocation so it can further its existence. From its perspective, it is satisfied as long as there is some engagement, whether it be obsessive, pathological, neurotic; or through trauma, pain, and suffering. The intriguing aspect is that the communal character disregards distinctions between love or pain, health or pathology; its relevance lies solely in captivating an individual's mind.

Essentially, it is an object made in human form, although it only represents it. The communal spirit in a given setting emphasizes strengths, while weaknesses, such as existential concerns and the standing of individuality, may not be seen as drawbacks by the wise. If anything, the centrality of being is the home base, and the existential situation motivates one toward progression and the future.

A totalitarian regime forms a collective group that represents the communal body to its fullest extent. Its entire structure, down to every detail, is an embodiment of the characteristics of any communal character in its purest form. It does not concern itself with individuality, viewing humanity as a numerical value. The regime operates under the principle of adhering to this communal identity, forfeiting individual existence to achieve the goal of progress.

The perceived maliciousness of such regimes often comes from their punishing commitment to the communal body, eliminating those who pose a threat to the system. Individuals seen as unwilling or incapable of strengthening the communal bond are labeled as threats. The actions of the collective become an embodiment of the communal character brought to life, with the observed hostility being something familiar to all of us. Beyond internal structures, the contemporary era imposes its own collective illusions—shaping identity in ways increasingly detached from biological or social roots.

SUSTAINING THE COMMUNAL CHARACTER

TO SUSTAIN the communal character it requires a synthesis of consciousness, interaction, and unity, without which the communal body dissolves into fragmentation or irrelevance.

FIRST: INTEGRATION WITHIN SOCIAL CONSCIOUSNESS

We cannot have a communal body that does not seek to integrate within the realm of human consciousness. Each member prerequisites to seek vitality and expansion from the group, which, in turn, allows for the creation of this communal character. When a communal body does not seek consciousness, or if its members are not interested in vitality or expansion, the communal body will begin to degenerate. For instance, if the majority of members of a communal body seek an existential state or enter a state of melancholy, they will weaken the entire conceptualization of the body.

In another instance, if the majority of members, or more precisely, the majority of influence—do not seek the expansion of consciousness and are contented with abandoning the state of progression, the communal body will weaken. However, this may not result in injury to the population, as it is natural to transition from a mode of progression to one of reflection and intimate development. This is a common response to delight, where an individual reflects on it in a state of uncertainty. Therefore, the communal body will follow a downward trend, which can be seen as a well repositioning.

SECOND: WILLINGNESS TO INTERACT

The communal body must be willing to interact with this communal character, even if it contains the aforementioned weaknesses. Principal among these flaws is that it does not fundamentally concern itself with any individual, not even the highest office, as history has shown us. The phrase "I didn't do it on purpose" reflects the occasion of individuality when the public has no recognition. We may want to find liability with the real public; however, they only represent the communal entity, and the delegates of these crowds do not represent themselves.

The same is true for one who studies statistics, which requires a detachment from the individuality for which the data represents in order to prompt a sophisticated level of study. The communal body requires its members to expense individuality so that each can interact with this communal character by means of an earnest mind. Had we granted a sense of individuality to it, we would disenfranchise those who could not relate to those specificities. Even a slight sense of humanness will come at a cost to its representation.

THIRD: INTERNAL UNITY

The communal body must be integrated, without divisiveness between individuals. This is because the communal character with whom each must interact must remain unified as a factual individual. When divisiveness occurs in the commonality of people, the communal character splits into two, with each representing a partiality of the community and expressing a form of individuality. The performance of true commonality becomes unavailable, and the communal character must take on social characteristics of individuality. This causes the communal body to regress towards proper individuality, devoid of any communal unity.

Thus, divisiveness within a communal body is the catalyst for individuals to attain true individuality. The more divisive it becomes, the more individualistic each member of the communal body develops to be. This grants individuality to each person as they attempt to interact with the communal entity, which begins to represent divisiveness—or, in other words, individuality.

In establishing its boundaries, the communal body must carefully regulate access to foreigners. Interaction with the communal character from an external perspective carries the risk of introducing individualistic elements. This immediately becomes a menace to the communal body, as the external party partakes in the portrayal of the communal character. A sense of individuality is introduced into the communal portrayal, thereby creating divisiveness that can destabilize the entire system.

This leads to a questionable notion of identity, which befalls by the existent stranger. As we have noted, certain divisiveness is healthy because it ensures vitality without allowing it to dissipate into irrelevance or external threats that could be existential. By remaining internal, the conflict itself ensures existential safety; as both sides agree on the wholeness of the communal body, even while claiming otherwise.

Therefore, every outsider to a communal body must be treated with mistrust and kept at a distance to discourage interaction with the communal body. The atmosphere upon entering a communal space—manifested through its setting— will confirm a certain distance between the outsider and the community, and vice versa. However, a communal body that is too stringent will not allow for expansive growth beyond its initial setting and will become unrelated to the broader global communal context, from which it derives its vitality.

Similar to an individual engaging with the communal body and relying on communal information for their individuality, the same principle applies to the communal body in relation to the comprehensive communal body. Every communal body depends on its larger counterpart, which is in turn dependent on the overarching communal body. Thus, the state, and the political sphere serves as the overarching communal body overhead every communal body within its borders. However, the state itself is dependent on the larger, universal communal body and must interact accordingly.

Therefore, every communal body operates on at least three levels: the first being itself, the second being the encompassing state, and the third being the universal communal entity. Certainly, additional levels are possible. For instance, a sub-domain of a religious identity would represent a specific component of its structure, with the second level being the overarching religious identity, the third being the state, and the fourth, the universal communal body. Between any communal body and its state, there can be sub-communal bodies, such as a city, neighborhood, or street.

When a communal body isolates itself from its overarching counterpart, it loses its prominence and vitality. When the communal body becomes detached from its greater entity, it becomes what we commonly define as a cult. A defining characteristic of cult-like behavior is a lack of deference for the communal body to which it belongs or for the entities overhead. The credibility of every communal body relies on its performance under the banner of its overarching communal body, with its only resolution as to disseminate greater information to a more intimate communal setting.

It's important to note that this belief is not a conscious choice made by the communal body. Instead, each individual remains attuned to a broader communal context. For each individual, only a single communal body can be attended at any given time. We cannot disenfranchise communal bodies and assert that we are engaged while disregarding the others. Communal bodies are not individualistic by nature; they encompass all communal space.

Thus, when someone engages with the state, they are also engaging with their familial body, their religious identity, and any other communal body they belong to. There are subconscious connections between these bodies. Just as an individual's habitat imparts communal information, the communal body is a habitat that offers a more intimate interaction with the incumbent communal bodies to which it serves.

When a communal body tries to deviate from this principle, it is urging its members to disconnect from their current perception of reality and behave as though the overarching communal entities do not exist. It also requests that connections to one's original communal settings—especially family—should not be part of their communal intimacy. If familial ties are allowed into this communal setting, every other communal body emerging from them must also be acknowledged.

The cult becomes isolated from all other communal bodies, much like an individual isolating themselves from communal settings. A cult differs from a communal body enacted with extreme vigilance—such as certain historical examples— since it does not respect reality. This differs from an individual who engages with the communal body with extreme fervor, like an avaricious person. It also differs from one who aligns with the communal body in a way distinct from its representation, such as a conspiracy theorist.

We can easily apply some of these ideas to contemporary political and social rhetoric concerning identity. However, such a task on my part would dilute the general nature of these sentiments, and thus, it is up to the reader to fill in the blanks according to their own interest

CONTAGIOUS IDENTITY

THE COMMUNAL BODY pursues a conceptualization so thoroughly embodied that individuals come to identify with the cause itself. Like a growing organism, it moves forward unchecked, consuming everything in its path—especially the bounded domain of selfhood, which is both the most accessible and the most precious. Without the natural resistance of individuality among its members, the communal potency will eventually ask the individual to internalize more and more of its collective identity.

This reminds us that the communal entity, like any decentralized system—be it a virus or mold—lacks an inherent conscience. It grows without reflection. Its only two prerequisites for expansion are a viable host and the absence of external resistance. Mold will grow indefinitely if the environment remains suitable and unchallenged. The same holds true for viruses, which spread through their hosts, progressing undeterred through biological systems. When we associate viral traits with intellectual behaviors, we symbolically point to collective characteristics that manifest under certain conditions.

This should not be confused with parasites, which have evolved to live in or on a host, causing harm—not as an intention, but as a consequence of their survival. The aim is not harm but survival as a biological entity. The host serves that purpose, forming a kind of symbiotic relationship in which the parasite benefits at the host's expense.

A virus, however, does not operate within any symbiotic framework and remains indifferent to whether the host succeeds or fails. This is quite extraordinary: even though its sole focus is to spread, the virus brings about the rapid decline of its host, which in turn leads to its own eventual decline. We might imagine that if the virus possessed any degree of sophistication, it would do well to ensure continuity in its host so that it could spread exponentially with a greater number of hosts. This is not the case, as it will only seek to manifest itself in its particular system. This would mean that it does not envision the possible spread of the near future, had it made a simple expense at the current moment to mediate its harm upon its host. The virus has no ability to neglect for a moment its tendency to spread. Even bacteria will host a certain symbiotic relationship, as is the case with gut microbiota, which comes to the aid of its hosts.

The only interaction viruses have with their hosts is the resistance they encounter, adapting in order to continue spreading. We might assume that with the ability to change its structure, a virus could theoretically choose to pause and thereby gain higher potency. Logically, halting movement appears less complex than restructuring an entire entity. However, to pause would require the virus to acknowledge a center—a point of reference on which to fall back. Movement cannot stop where there is no location from which to rest, even temporarily.

In this sense, a *destination* implies the virus envisions an endpoint that requires subsequent steps to reach. But a virus cannot envision finality, or even recognize the foreseeable future. It doesn't aim for a second position; rather, it is wholly absorbed in the immediacy of its next move. The single movement as its only motion. That small movement is considered its final destination, which requires an array of minuscule movements to get there.

The virus is exhibiting a low form of complexity, which seems like an inconsistent formula for conquering all living life. Rather, it is only seeking to elicit a minor change, which cannot be envisioned beyond or around that. It is viral because it is simple and doesn't apply itself to the rules of generality and complexity. There is a minuscule center for a virus, but it is utterly engaged with its subsequent movement.

We can define the communal body in the same, which contains a minuscule center—though not one akin to a self, as it never shifts focus away from its subsequent minor step. The vision of a communal body is so fundamentally simple and momentary that it appears to lack purpose—except to spread. As with the virus, the observable goal of the communal body is to proliferate. We observe its myriad movements and interpret them as evidence of a systematic spread. Yet there is no actual system in place to support the information required to initiate such spread.

If, from the moment of inception, it encompasses a destination, a trajectory toward it, and a central point through which the information can be disseminated. When we don't find these traits, we can assume that the problem with the virus is such that it is too simple for complex organisms and subsequent intellectuality.

The harm of a virus is that it doesn't interact in a symbiotic relationship with its hosts, particularly because it does not contain the complexity to do so. As the virus becomes more complex, it will envision more of its movements. With such development of greater movements, it will require a center housing its progress. Analogous to a human with a single step, there is no prerequisite for a destination or an initial point.

Twenty steps would require precision in their aim for all those movements, thereby a centered mindset which would continuously disseminate information for each of the twenty.

If we are being precise, even a single step contains a destination and a center, with embedded minuscule movements that constitute the whole step. Every movement regularly requires a central base to continuously direct its function which originates from a location that is inherently removed—both materially and cognitively—from the command. The movement itself cannot perform the movement, for it is solely engaged with the process of moving.

If we were to extract the 'movement' from the elements that participate in it, we would find a receptor with a point to receive information, while the rest serve the sole purpose of enacting that information in the form of movement. The connection between the 'enactor' and the 'receptor' is itself an enactment.

For instance, a person who takes a trip to a destination sees the trip as 'movement.' This movement is actuated by the command to perform it. In terms of the movement itself—the trip—it contains no trait other than to enact the idea as movement. The transmission from the idea to movement is part of the movement, which is constantly enacting itself, unto which the idea has tapped.

We can perceive movement as continuously being enacted to perform itself, with the idea entering and constraining contained by certain parameters. There was always the trip in existence, but the traveler narrows it to be from one point to another. As for the 'trip,' it remains as it always is, while the person concludes to be a trip to a specific destination. The body can be considered as moving in all possible ways at all times, which is then constrained by a central command concerning specific tasks.

This is why one cannot move a hand steadily across; it will be better suited when there is tension or resistance. When moving the hand alone, it seeks the complete range of its motions, allocated to pursue its natural state. To be calm and collected is antithetical to the body's natural state, while being chaotic and erratic is its natural manifestation. When the mind loses cognitive control, as in the case with certain patients, the body begins to move in its natural form.

The art of dance makes use of both the erratic chaos of bodily movements and a cognitive system that imposes parameters upon it. Most artists will tell you that there is disorder, which then gets restricted into an art form. Movement is the manner of existence, and quiet and calm are illusions concerning that. The mind that controls the body to halt all movements incorporates the many movements of the body into its structure.

Therefore, the mind of the person meditating is orchestrating the movements that restrain the body. This is the peculiar ability of nature *to replace movement with movement*. When we constrain the 'meta format of the *trip*' to a single trip to a specific destination, the constricting process is a higher movement which has taken over a weaker one.

The mind contains both a higher quantity and quality of movement, which can surpass weaker forms of movement. It is not the strength of a movement that makes it dominant, but rather the fact that movement naturally follows the stronger current. When we consider all movement as allocated to a single current, which is then divided into smaller currents, it follows that when movements interact, and they align with the stronger current.

When the brain is damaged and simple motor movements fail, it is not due to a structural issue per se, but because the central command to perform movements has been impaired. Had a healthy central command remained, even with structural issues, it would have adapted and found a way to improvise through plasticity as necessary.

When a substantial number of movements are added to a situation, a more complex base is required to continuously interact with each of them. Individuality emerges where more "movements" are envisioned in one's life; the more movements there are, the more individualistic one becomes. Measuring the number of movements corresponds to the level of complexity regarding movements. Movements that interact with others possess a dual sense of movement, with the interaction always counted as a movement in itself, alongside the others. For example, a material sport requires a significant number of movements to perform the skill. However, even as those movements are developed with precision, which constitutes a complete set of movements, they pale in comparison to cognitive disciplines.

When an individual studies a discipline, the mind engages not only in distinct movements toward the material but also between and around the material. If each thought is considered a movement, then a mental discipline contains an astronomically greater number of movements than material activity. When twenty steps are set toward a goal, they contain a specific number of steps. But if all twenty steps interact with each other while attempting to reach the destination, then each step becomes incalculable. When there is an additional reflection on the twenty steps, the entire process is doubled, and so on.

A virus is an entity that does nothing more than its next move, becoming a threat to any biological system. Essentially, it is a form of movement so simple that it moves without detection. Because of its simplicity, it is not recognized as subordinate to the stronger streams of movement. It becomes inaccessible as a movement being so trivial that larger hosts, with their larger strides of change cannot distinguish it from the background.

The virus is a constrained version of movement, like any entity in nature, but with an overly basic form of central command and autonomy. Higher modes of movement must be able to discern that level of simplicity, even while dealing with particular complexity. The virus mobilizes by virtue of greater movements having no ability to identify or integrate with such forms of simplicity.

This principle extends to the communal body functioning in a similar manner. Its power of mobilization lies in its simplicity as a formulation. This goes unnoticed or unchallenged because people either do not acknowledge its existence or are unable to cope with such a simplistic formula. Communal energy is so transparent within the nature of social engagements and so simple that it cannot be broken, conceding its power. It contains no complex motivation other than the mere transition to another single point, and for human interaction, that can be easily dispersed. It is no coincidence that the more one attaches to a communal body, the less sophisticated and complex they become.

What is happening is that organisms of absolute complexity are entering a domain that operates on a scale of simplicity. One may inquire about the possibility of an organism entering a more elemental area than that of a virus. However, due to its inherent incompatibility, it fails to become an obstacle. Similar to a fly, which does not evoke human emotions in the same way a dog might. What gives the virus its ability to become an obstacle, containing nothing that would make it compatible with a complex organism?

Furthermore, how can a communal body exist, having built its conceptualization against human reliability? In reality, the virus flourishes only because of the communal body to which it relates. If we were to eliminate the entire communal conceptualization from all societies—including the notion of 'society'—we would likely not find widespread viral spread. The more important question is: what about the communal entity is relatable to human interaction?

We find many attachments to the communal entity giving a sense of realness: a library of complexity, existential safety, disciplines to discern information, a sense of intimacy, and others. All of these benefits are not inherently communal and can be performed well without the communal sense. What makes the communal entity truly relatable is the simplistic movement to that one single point. Essentially, what inclines people toward it is *a nostalgic sentiment of regressing to when life was simple.*

This is the relatable item upon which all other benefits stand. In our subjective experience, though interacting with the collective, the item that reflects upon ourselves is that simplistic viral structure of a single movement without knowledge of the future or surrounding context. When an able-bodied person fixatedly adheres to a communal entity, they do so to obtain the experience of the non-complex life form and the *freedom of the virus.*

This highlights the paradox of civilization, which, despite its grandeur, often undermines the complexity of life forms. We might feel compelled to reverse this dynamic, removing the constraints of civilization, especially when it conflicts with the richness of life itself.

In contrast to the intricate nature of intimate relationships or complex theories, a model that prioritizes only immediate, localized actions lacks the depth to compete. It is laden with unrelatable features, more akin to an object than a human. Such a conceptualization should, in theory, be no match for a progressive mindset. However, this is not the case, as it often operates under the radar or becomes obscured by vague linguistic terms (e.g., society, the public).

As we've noted, emotional attachments are deeply rooted, beginning with our interactions within the original family unit. However, this emotional bond does not justify the conceptual simplicity or limited relatability often associated with it. We are left with something profoundly sentimental, yet arguably weaker than even the simplest theory. There must surely be a willingness to confront this disturbance without allowing it to overshadow our capacity for nuance. Like a virus, the challenge lies in recognizing it—it appears omnipresent, yet when we attempt to pinpoint it, it seems to vanish.

There also appears to be something within the communal body that functions at a relatively basic level, possibly because conceptual complexity becomes diluted when stretched across a large number of people. Each individual tied to a communal identity may unintentionally contribute to a reduction in its depth. Paradoxically, the more proponents involved in constructing a shared human experience, the more we see a divergence from the uniqueness of individual human experience.

The collective body, in this sense, resembles a virus embedded in the structure of every communal entity. The concern isn't with a particular group, but only to the lack of individual resistance toward its claim on introspective mental capacities. The informational material has gone *viral* as the individual embodiment of a political entity has reached a degree where we would consider the mind unable to resist informational ingestion.

When that occurs, the individual will have placed the entire biological system as a device to integrate a deeper awareness of the communal body. They may feel they cannot fully understand themselves without engaging the demands of identity. Religious identity often benefits from this dynamic, presenting itself as a necessary framework for self-understanding. When this is internalized, the conceptualization gains access to personal vulnerabilities, reinforcing itself further.

Interestingly, the identity of a state does not pursue this level of embodiment as fervently as religious identity tends to. One possible reason is that, when fully merged with identity, the state loses the flexibility required to function effectively. While religious identity may remain unconcerned with political or practical concerns, a state that departs from them risks becoming extraneous.

Moreover, a state circumvents its citizens becoming preoccupied with its conceptualization to prevent a heightened state of revolutionary spirit. Because it must deal with the true political present-day, an over-engagement of the populace will invariably lead to revolution or anarchy. Whenever the notion is absolutely practical and political, any extreme movements will undermine the democratic structure.

Democracy relies on its lethargic movements to filter out the aggressiveness of certain notions, repeatedly seeking to form a balance of the extremities. Ideas that enter into the state's periphery instantaneously become actionable, and a populace who absolutely identifies with the state will input a vast array of pseudo-developed ideas. Not only will they become actionable, but they will encompass a populace who cannot differentiate the state's ideas from their intrinsic realm.

Nationalism consistently overlooks such issues, operating under the assumption that all collective bodies can be treated identically. The truth of the matter is that, depending on the degree of political energization that a collective body has, that would be the criteria for effectuating an absolute embodiment of the conceptualization.

We can identify a populace that has embodied the state's identity as if it were a religious construct by its actions when the state is existentially tested. When we find individuals experiencing individual existential disarray alongside the state, we can be sure that there is an absolute embodiment. They cannot distinguish a part of their respective estate which is not accompanying the state, thereby causing them to follow the movements of the state with the patterns of their breath.

When the conceptualization becomes embodied to a certain degree, complexity is narrowed and becomes a skeletal version of itself. This was evident in the Middle Ages, when intensified identity embodiment led to executions and wars driven more by ideology than by territorial gain. Yet through all this embodiment, we don't find a vast array of complexity attributed to those identities.

This decline in complexity arises from identity occupying increasing biological territory, with the mind—a primary source of complexity—carried along in the process. While complexity undoubtedly persisted, as it does throughout nature, there were few neutral or reflective perspectives capable of discerning it.

This leads us to the conclusion that any form of embodiment would be detrimental to sophistication. And that would be incorrect, for at intervals, a slight form of ritualistic embodiment can allow information to resonate more deeply with selfhood. Without any embodiment, we risk remaining mere observers, never fully engaging. Participation allows observation to become both accurate and intimate. Becoming the spectacle loses the entire observation, which also causes all choices to be inconsistent and cyclical.

MAINTAINING THE COMMUNAL BODY

THE COMMUNAL BODY resists simple definition because it spans multiple inherently collective dimensions—economic competence, confidence (or courage), and political or social traits. Economic activity presupposes at least two parties; confidence exists only insofar as it is perceived by another. Likewise, political and social life are built on interactions among many individuals. Because these characteristics depend on relationships among two or more agents, they belong to the communal sphere. Moreover, information itself emerges in the shared space between participants, transcending any single individual's limitations and assuming a communal form.

Whenever one engages with any of these domains, they interact with a communal body—not an isolated individual. No single person interfaces with the political system, the economy, or the social realm as a sequestered entity. The very notion of competence exists only through the recognition of others. In primordial times, competence consisted of hunter-gatherer skills; today, it encompasses understanding complex social systems. Just as relating to another individual reflects aspects of the self, engaging with the communal body reflects communal dimensions of one's identity.

There is nothing inherent within an individual that corresponds directly to this non-individualistic entity. One must carve out a niche of communal representation that overlays the personal psyche. We can understand this niche as a function of the superego, which connects the communal dimension to the individual core through various psychological links.

We become bound to the communal notion by virtue of being raised within it. The family unit is communal in its properties. We often notice this most clearly during conflict, when family members assert individual autonomy against that collective. Until those moments, a cohesive bond endures. The family embodies communal traits—above all, a disregard for individual autonomy. Though this may be concealed, when the family as a whole gains broader recognition, its communal inclination becomes apparent.

Our initial attachment to the family underpins all later communal relationships. When that primary bond weakens, our connections to other communal bodies also falter. Assigning greater significance to a single communal body inevitably recalls primary family experiences—and vice versa. This reciprocity is especially vivid in artists or public figures: as they engage more deeply with wider communities, memories of the primal family often resurface with sharper relief.

Engaging with the communal body is inherently unstable. On one side stands the individual, with defined traits and experiences; on the other, an entity without singular specificity yet more complex. To discern its intricacies, we must observe interactions among many individuals—sometimes even a small group can generate immense connotations. The hazard is twofold: the individual may be swept into this complexity and lose personal distinction, or may project imagined complexity onto their own individuality.

Some attempt to reshape the social environment to serve their individualistic needs, interacting only with reflections of themselves while engaging the communal body. Yet this misapprehends the nature of that body, which differs fundamentally from the individual. Such restructuring becomes a mirror of their self-perception: rather than expressing their authentic self, they reshape the environment to embody that version.

Although integration can be valuable at times, losing oneself in the communal body without reclaiming individuality is problematic. Such individuals skip essential steps—first establishing proper interaction, then rushing into unification—disallowing a genuine relationship to form. As a result, they leave themselves vulnerable to being completely engulfed by the collective.

Conversely, some readily succumb to the communal body and gradually lose their sense of self. They begin to identify solely as representatives of the communal system. This constitutes a form of individualistic demise: the longer it endures, the harder it becomes to reclaim one's individuality, since numerous crucial steps have been neglected.

The challenge lies in retaining individuality while interacting with something complex which lacks individual traits. This demands a high level of personal development to navigate the environment without becoming lost in its network. Engaging dynamically with the communal body illustrates that the individual is advanced—possessing the fortitude to maintain inner substantiation. Achieving this requires significant experience, time, and incremental progress toward proper interaction.

One can quickly enter the communal sphere and become lost within it, especially since the communal body is made up of individuals who either represent or appear to demand conformity. However, in times of serious crisis or significant events, the communal identity of these representatives often fades. In societies overly immersed in communal bodies, we cannot assume that individuals lack intimacy or nuance.

Sustained engagement with the collective rarely coexists with personal intimacy: the collective offers only fragments of intimacy compared to sincere one-on-one relationships. The more an individual interacts without an individualistic framework, the more they form immaterial or unfounded assumptions about it. Without an individual lens to process this data, one cannot grasp the communal body's complex structure; one's understanding becomes impossible.

We often observe two flawed perspectives in such individuals. First, they exclude themselves from the judgments they make about the communal; second, they believe the communal body wields direct power over specific lives. Both perspectives share a common flaw: a lack of an individual framework with which to process the communal body.

The first perspective may yield coherent judgments but lacks a practical foundation for how a person in an actual scenario would interact or manage. The second projects resentment, stemming from dependence upon the communal body and the belief that it is responsible for their loss of individuality. This stance lacks intellectual stimulation and represents a misdirection in personal development. While individualization is necessary, these individuals find culpability with the communal body for its absence. The only probable benefit of this stance is its simplicity, which may render such individuals more adaptable to sudden shifts that lead back to selfhood.

By contrast, the first perspective becomes highly stimulated by its intellectual engagement with the communal body and will not swiftly shift toward intimacy and selfhood. Though adherents gain a form of moral development from their judgments, these often falter in practice. This divergence from practicality compels such individuals to seek refuge in theoretical systems that perpetuate the impression of individual absence.

During this intellectual refuge, they may acquire extensive knowledge—knowledge worthy of incorporation into society. This reinforces their status as refugees: while society may benefit from their contributions, their subjective experience becomes mislaid. Fundamentally defective theories arise, embodying their personal failure to engage effectively with the communal body and its knowledge.

The notion of *one-size-fits-all* does not apply; instead, ideas serve those who fit them. The metaphor of having "no shoes" reflects self-identification as omnipresent, as though one need not engage personhood during judgment. But what kind of omnipresence is it if judgment exists in a realm that cannot be practically engaged?

Judgment serves to safeguard and advance consciousness, securing its continuity across time. In this perspective, judgment matters only to the extent that it furthers the development and preservation of consciousness—which itself rests on ongoing personal growth. Every individual possesses a certain degree of consciousness, and society as a whole reflects the average of these varying degrees. Because consciousness emerges from subjective human experiences, the more complex a person becomes, the more nuanced their judgments will be.

INTEGRATION, DOUBT, AND UNIFICATION

Consciousness is objectively based, yet its maintenance is subjective. A fully developed consciousness does not necessitate judgment, for everything is intuitively understood in the transparency of that awareness. When transparency is lacking, the strides made are vulnerable to being lost.

There are no judgments in realms of complete transparency. For instance, we do not question whether we have bodies—the notion is universally evident. Even in the face of scientific doubt, with such inquiries, the objective is to deepen our awareness—not to claim we've lost consciousness of that domain, but to seek greater understanding upon a foundation already made clear through tradition.

This is the process of all learning: at advanced levels, the preceding level is temporarily questioned. Ultimately, unification occurs—integrating both the former and latter stages into a comprehensive whole. The period of doubt is permanently etched in time and cannot be erased from our mental periphery. At any moment, one can abandon the advanced level and return to past models as though no progress has been made. If progress has truly occurred, only unification can make such a return significant.

The moment one retreats into an earlier context while carrying unresolved material from the next level is the most precarious point in mastering knowledge. In that interval, one is suspended between two levels—unable to be fully extracted from either. The advanced level has been abandoned, and the previous one is not yet integrated with the new insights. The only solution in this realm is integration: the weaving together both levels to create a comprehensive and coherent picture.

INDIVIDUALITY AND THE COMMUNAL BODY

While certain communal bodies resist forming a persona contrary to their nature—and others struggle with how communal interaction challenges their humanness—people persist in treating the collective as if it consists of individual beings. Individuals within the collective are not only viewed as abstractions but as embodiments of the community in its entirety.

This occurs because individuals seek individualism in every engagement. When it is obligatory to deal with a collective, they are dissatisfied with its lack of individuality. As a result, they search for individuality where it does not inherently exist, extracting human sentimentally to serve as sanctuaries for public engagement. This process is often unconscious. Every encounter with the collective becomes a stage upon which individuality must be discovered.

We might then ask: Is the reverse possible? Could the collective willingly adopt an individualistic persona and demand reciprocal individualistic engagement? And if so, why would a collective concern itself with the trivialities of personal lives, given its inherently communal orientation?

Nonetheless the collective can be infused with whatever theories its constituents construct. This may lead to the communal entity adopting an individualistic persona—with intent to engage as though it were made of flesh and blood.

This puts the individual in a precarious position. Society may begin to function like a correctional facility, demanding that individuals interact with a system that enforces human-like engagement while lacking definite human vulnerability. There is no purpose in resisting this imposition of individualism by the collective; it is omnipresent and invulnerable, unlike a person, who could be wounded or defeated.

Those who claim otherwise are operating under a misconception, as even if their trifling actions leave a mark on the communal body, that organization does not experience such a stain as a wound. The communal entity will degenerate without pain or concern, although we project human characteristics so that we can engage in variance—like trying to defeat an inanimate object.

Accepting this reality offers no reliable solution either, for in doing so, one eventually becomes an embodiment of the collective by engaging with an aspect that contradicts their human nature. With enough exposure to the collective, they may eventually internalize such, with only a trace of resentment to remind them of their humanness.

The only viable approach when confined by their parameters is to engage with the collective as a factual collective construct, even when it disguises itself as individualistic. When individual manifestations appear within the collective, they should be dismissed as impressions. This demands an understanding of what a collective truly is, as well as an introspective awareness of our emotional attachments to communal aspects—particularly those rooted in family.

Even when individuals sincerely claim to embody the collective and expect to be treated accordingly, the populace recognizes they are merely enacting it. Yet, within that enactment, some trace of human nature remains. Recognizing this requires complex psychological and philosophical insight.

Despite the collective's denial of individuality, its defining feature is its lack of a self. There is no center upon which the state rests. A ruler may be appointed to represent the collective, but even within that ruler's subjectivity, there is only partial individuality and partial adherence to that communal role.

Regarding the familial body, the relationship between parents is itself a communal entity. From the parents' perspectives, this relationship may feel individualistic, however, to the children, it is experienced communally. No individual within the relationship exists as such for the child. Each parent may have a personal relationship with the child, but the relationship between the parents is experienced as a communal system.

What unfolds within the parental relationship contributes to the complexity of a child's familial experience. This dynamic becomes a stage for the most intimate emotional developments. Children are biological manifestations of the individual parents—not of their relationship. No biological component within the child originates from the relationship itself. As the child matures, they begin to conceptualize the parental relationship, often forming their first understanding of a communal body. Through interaction with this concept, they begin to shape their individual track.

When parents are hostile, the child experiences the relationship much like one would a dysfunctional communal body. The child may identify with one parent and develop an individualistic framework, but their engagement with the relationship itself mirrors a descent into a deteriorating communal environment. A communal body in decline signals dysfunction: hostility reveals division, weakening cohesion, while individuality surfaces.

This helps explain why a child might take the side of one parent—the communal unity of the relationship is dissolving, exposing each parent more clearly as a separate individual. The child is then compelled to confront the unmediated reality of each parent's personality, once veiled by the communal structure of their relationship.

One purpose of a communal entity is to shield us from full exposure to raw individuality. While this may seem stifling, it actually serves to protect developing psyches. For a child to witness their parents for the employed personal detail is to confront the full weight of their own developing self. Overexposure to the raw self can cause stagnation—paralysis in the face of too much complexity. Even adults can become unmoored, when exposed too quickly to the dissolution of communal systems, may become unmoored, unable to process the flood of internal information.

From this perspective, schizophrenics may be understood as individuals who have departed from the communal body and plunged too deeply into their own unrestrained individuality. Their condition reveals a kind of overexposure, resulting in confusion and stagnation. We should pay attention to the content of their experience—they confront a more complete form of individuality. Yet we also need communal structures to temper this exposure. A gradual emergence into selfhood is essential.

Terms like "soul-crushing" often describe the oppressive side of communal life. While this may seem like a loss of humanity, paradoxically, it prevents the devastation that too much "soul" might inflict if revealed all at once. However, failing to cultivate distinctiveness within a communal structure can feel just as terminal.

This failure is not the fault of the community, which itself holds neither virtue nor vice. Any person can escape the communal body. We see this in schizophrenics, who disengage from it regardless of their environment. The institution that houses them is a communal entity disturbed by the intensity of their individuality. And yet, even within confinement, they don't dissolve into the collective—they plunge deeper into themselves. Ironically, the institution may help them by offering containment through which more of the self can be expressed in structured form.

Perhaps the solution is not more structure, but environments even more individualistic than they are—such as remote or underdeveloped communities. Cities are often the worst environments for those struggling with excessive individuality. Yet, paradoxically, they seek refuge there, hoping the strict communal framework will temper their inner disorder. A more remote setting, however, might offer genuine healing.

Among others who are deeply engaged with their own individuality, they may begin to reflect on their condition and become self-conscious of their disarray. I've seen this firsthand in a remote suburb, where individuals with serious issues showed remarkable improvement over time. One man, who had spent his days drinking on a bench, speaking incoherently, sleeping in parks, and neglecting hygiene, began reading sophisticated texts, took part in respectful communal work, and replaced alcohol with water. Another person left the park bench behind and became socially active. A third, who had leaned toward troubling mental habits like talking to himself or mingling exclusively with the mentally challenged, found friends of similar nature and functioned well. A fourth, previously estranged from a large family and aimless, began dressing well and participating in society. A fifth, partially schizophrenic and prone to dissociation, left town—perhaps to avoid the positive changes taking place.

When I first arrived, I assumed mentally challenged individuals would be at risk without the city's institutional support. Quite the opposite occurred. I have not met a single individual in that environment who didn't, in some way, find respite and adapt meaningfully to society. Through all these encounters, it seems almost impossible not to achieve some measure of mental stability in such a setting.

Such an environment should not be civilized in the sense that a communal body is overtly structured. Nor should it have officials who assume roles of communal dissemination—no despotic rulers or mystical healers. It must be *uncivilized* in the sense that the communal body is not visibly or structurally represented, yet it must still be a communal entity—though not a tribal one. In tribal settings, there would be no real interaction between the communal entity and the mentally challenged individual; they would remain inaccessible to one another. I speak instead of a communal body that does not appear as such to its members—free, but composed.

The communal body does not aim to suppress individuality any more than an object cares about its user. It simply seeks to exist and persist—and for that, individuals must make themselves available. Even this impulse is not the collective's, but belongs to the individuals who comprise it.

The same is true of the parental relationship. It "seeks" to maintain itself by absorbing the communal sensibilities of spouses and their social surroundings. It doesn't care about morality or outcomes. It functions only by attaching itself to the communal dimension internalized by those involved. When a child observes their parents' relationship, they encounter both emotional weight and the absence of personal concern. Even if the relationship is visible, it only affects the child if they sense its communal essence.

INTIMACY, INDIVIDUALITY, AND THE COMMUNAL BODY

We cannot have a relationship with another person without a coinciding communal attachment that solidifies the relationship as a conceptual reality. This explains why most relationships are built from—or through—familial or communal bodies. We can connect in a relatable manner from one person to another, without any communal interference. However, a child—or anybody, for that matter—cannot distinguish that sensibility of connection without a communal manifestation that houses that sentiment.

For instance, if one spouse intimately touches another, it is an act embedded in both individualistic and communal aspects. The visibility of bodily interactions to society brings forth that intimate experience, aligning it with the communal atmosphere. Moreover, within the subjective experience of each spouse—even under the presumption that no one can possibly observe their interaction—they would derive some form of intimacy from a communal aspect. It occurs as if the world were watching and participating, even as they depart into intimate materiality.

Without communal representation as part of that intimate interaction, there would be no feeling of intimacy—for they would be merely individuals in a nonexistent world. Every interaction would be considered intimate, thus making all interactions non-intimate. The reason certain connections feel more intimate than others is that the communal environment interacts more stalwartly with some and less so with others. Without any communal interaction, there is no external resistance to define what is to be considered intimate.

A mentally challenged individual, especially one who departs from the communal body, may be unaware of the degrees of intimacy coinciding within themselves. Certainly, there may be remnants of recognition regarding their sexual aspects—and with that, an intuitive guardedness toward more intimate regions. However, the more they depart from the communal front—as in the case of the feral man—the more they become unashamed of being naked, viewing the differing regions of their body as essentially the same.

Intimacy is intricately linked to the communal body from which it seeks to depart. Individuals who are secluded, both materially and mentally from the communal body will be unable to perform even a simplistic intimate gesture. Anecdotally, we find that intimate gestures are more common when people are nearby. In the complete privation of the communal body, such gestures become less frequent. The same applies to sexual interaction, which diminishes for those emotionally and materially detached from the communal body.

People exposed to intimate interactions often perceive them as they would when observing a nearby couple. While it may seem like an intimate experience for the observer, it is, in fact, a communal experience for those involved. This dynamic also applies to pornography, which, despite its seemingly personal nature, is inherently communal and reveals intimacy as a significant form of artistic expression.

Consequently, there emerges a sentiment of glorification toward the viewed imagery. When intimacy is translated into a communal setting, it becomes an art form. For the couple themselves, in the interior of the individualistic components of their experience, intimacy is felt in weaker proportions. As the proverb goes, "Better is the sight of the eyes than the experience of desire."

The community remains stimulating as a displayed version of intimacy, allowing interaction without the repercussions of true intimacy affecting the subjective experience. It becomes communal—bottled into a substance that can be appreciated while remaining non-individualistic and detached from real engagement.

This parallels violence, which has been politicized—i.e., communalized—to respect individual intimacy and the subsequent loss of life. It seems to be an intimate interaction between lives, albeit politicized for the communal protection of the individual. Yet upon further scrutiny, we find that the politicized entity—or the communal sentiment—is uncaring about us as individuals, unlike a true relationship. However, engaging in politicized violence will not lead to reciprocity; instead, it will be ignored.

This becomes ironic because politicized violence attempts to place the individual on a pedestal for recognition, luring engagement under the presumption of individualism, while ultimately risking the loss of true individuality. This is not necessarily troubling, for we are indebted to The Enlightenment for teaching us individuality—ironically, a communal body that has given us a sense of ourselves. However, those who were successful in that endeavor were coupled to the communal body for a certain interval before subsequently disengaging to truly reflect on their innate individuality, which is inaccessible within the communal body.

When children somehow gain a sense of individuality, they begin to disconnect from the relational material of their parents and treat each one as a bare individual. This, in turn, threatens the relationship of the parents, which relies on the ambiguity of their connection. This mirrors a constant threat in art—exposing the non-enlightening background that produced the art form. When we discover actors, poets, or artists who are painfully human and unremarkable in their orientation, the art they produce develops to be uninteresting. The ambiguous nature of art is its lifeline; when we uncover the humanistic traits behind it, the art loses its communal sense and becomes individualistic.

Children who identify their parents as isolated entities cause the parents to internalize such a perception. The same principle applies to any communal body, such as the state. If citizens gain a sense of individuality beyond what is necessary, the state begins to lose its conceptualization and thus degenerate. This contributes to the eventual decline of civilizations: members inevitably develop on an individual basis, disrupting the state's symbolic integrity. This can materialize in two ways: either individuals obtain their individuality by force, akin to a child in a divorced family, or naturally gain more selfhood, diminishing the necessity of the state's overarching protection.

Even in a state occupied by intellectuals, the matter of the next generation persists. We are reminded of the Greeks, who did not revere the next generation, as reflected in their attachment to pederasty. While one may not need the state's amenities to protect the humanity, the familial body will usually require such protection. Children cannot gain entrance into specific individuality solely because their parents have done so. Individuals must redo the work and engage with the communal environment across an extended period before experiencing incremental change.

Intellectuals, upon self-reflection, may discover that achieving individuality is challenging short of the support of society and the state. Even at the highest peak of vigorous individuality, they will usually require some communal protection for their vulnerable moments—or, at the very least, in their engagements with the social environment, particularly the family.

Those who have gained individuality will recognize their continued reliance on the communal body for information. If anything, they would reintegrate with the communal body to help shape conversation and culture. Achieving individuality removed from the communal setting still retains remnants of a dated communal interest. We are tethered to the communal body because it holds a complexity that no single individual can contain. Through such a library of complexity, the path to deeper individuality is paved by an even more rigorous engagement.

A feral man will inevitably assimilate into animal culture due to the inability to retain human information independently. Even effortlessly absorbing the entirety of human knowledge may not foster relatability or contribute to individuality. A physicist, for instance, must adhere to that discipline to contribute meaningfully to society. They must embody that role and become a physicist. Such engagement produces substantial benefits for the collective body. Each member does the same, contributing to a vast and evolving communal library.

It is unworkable for a single human to embody numerous roles simultaneously unless each is specifically configured for a singular role. Such entities would also require individualistic characteristics to relate to themselves, demanding a degree of autonomy. Because an artificial substructure is inanimate, it fundamentally relates to the non-animacy of itself. Human substructure, by contrast, is animate: each part is an organism in itself.

PUBLIC SPEECH AND MATERIALITY

CONVERSATION and its various modalities are thought to be encased in private affairs, only seeping into the public sphere when necessary or at the brim of frustration. The prevalent wisdom is that any encounter requiring public effect is already at the site of activity—and there is much merit to such an argument.

For one, the public is politically noticed, so that infrastructure and its representations take foremost notice, such is the sociality in their expression of activity. It would seem futile to mount any countermeasure when infrastructure is concrete—like the division of states or the independence of another—all in all, forms of attempted change without an exemplification of infrastructure.

This may be circumvented by displaying a party slogan, so that the thoroughfares are filled with that change, yet this alone serves to exemplify its discrepancy—like how a state must advertise its legitimacy approximating a corporation, or as some attempt at a genuine process. Taken from the Roman legions, or other traditions in which banners are used to give a form of recognition, they are meant for morale or bureaucratic distinction rather than for recognition of infrastructure itself.

Rome and its armies did not require banners to establish legitimacy; when employed, such symbols functioned less as nostalgic re-enactments and more as formal identifiers—akin to the header of a document indicating the authority under which an agreement is made—a secondary imprint of an already secured sovereignty, devoid of theatrical display.

Secondly, the transfer of change is readily the change of infrastructure, occurring within the realm of activity—whether by war or by reconfiguration. We may even accept that war is the primary form of creation and recreation of a state, simply because it is active, not conversed. It embodies action without many words, and its aftermath is negotiation. This is why taxes are such a lewd point in all statehood—not for the mere loss of currency, which certainly has merit—but because it is the moment in which statehood enters the residency of private affairs to negotiate its terms.

While other exemplifications of statehood, such as military or policing, are surely tied to infrastructure and noticed in the thoroughfares, these serve specific objectives that the law-abiding citizen does not usually encounter. For even the law-abiding citizen, the moment of intersection with the political arena lies in either departure or entrance to such a locality, and taxation—such that, if one were not to depart nor owe any tax, there would be no direct interaction between individual and state.

Particular actions to which the state pays greater attention—such as weapon wielding or complex instrument use—form another point of intersection, necessitating increased policing due to the potential for devastation. Children or other familial dependents constitute yet another form of state oversight—granting power to a dependency—but only after the individual has chosen to embark upon that venture. Because necessity is tied to economy, taxation remains ever-present, unlike the aforementioned intersections.

Third, the representee and their persuasive speech depend on the acceptance of both their own supporters and those of the opposing representee—an alignment that typically reflects not objective reality, but the shifting whims of individuals. A public cannot speak—only individuals can—and the words of an individual are not the enumeration of the public, but rather their private interpretation of some public sentiment. Therefore, the activity of the public is most true to that particular public, because it does not become a display of its properties, but the expression itself.

The same is observed in the regulation of any organization, especially the familial body. Where materiality is absent—as in the case of the affluent, where services substitute for structure—the division of materiality usurps the modality of the organization, and is experienced without the political reverence accompanying such a structure. Materiality is the manner of expression that gives political relevance; it is the negative effect behind materially charged domestic disputes, which freeload that process when utility is not otherwise organized.

Speech is found to be somewhat futile in the context of public communication—whether to its own citizens or in diplomacy. Yet speech is also the process through which all materiality is taken into the mode of conceptual reintegration. This is why we must find a manner of performing speech that avoids the aforementioned negative attributes and instead lends political relevance.

There are two forms to this process. One is the speech that precedes action—the last parley before war—given substance by its proximity to the sacrifice and detriment of conflict. Yet, because it already lies within the sphere of accepted battle, any agreement still bears the mark of mobilized materiality, awaiting expression in another form.

This is another reason strong negotiation is problematic: the leverage is placed on the table, and all detriment is accepted as a real possibility until resolution is found. However, since the negotiating parties have already accepted the furthest degeneration, it remains embedded in the final terms, awaiting future expression.

For example, blackmail may be effective in achieving results, yet, because the parties do not want the terms of the negotiation but accept them for the real notice of further degeneration, the terms themselves will be constituted with the embedded detriment, and thus both parties will attempt to see to it that they create a counter response—on one side to retaliate the revenge the usage of a conceptual undercut, and on the other because they have usurped power in terms that are contingent on the vulnerability of another.

There is another manner of accessing speech in political form: bureaucratic insistence on constant communication, whereby so much speech falls into a continuous stream that, by the sheer volume of the process, both parties—whether the public or the diplomatic end—engage with it as though the speech were politically relevant and receive its substance as an element of infrastructure.

We will use a highly charged example: live televised events that are accepted as infrastructure—such as the moon landing—which leave a deep imprint on society, comparable to the impact of fully realized warfare in terms of political relevance. It is precisely because of these elements that they hold such significance. It bore the constant communication leading to the result, whether by its inception in historical imaginings of such an occurrence, or its daily practice and conversments leading up to that decade. The gathering of all this communication reached its conversational climax and achieved its objective. That culmination created the impact it had. If there had been limited conversation—whether public or private—even a more revolutionary event would have had less effect.

Primarily, it is the conversing and its culmination—with nations and individuals participating in its detail—that gave the final result such impact. Continuous communication, even when like-minded from one instance to the next, gains credence through connection more than content. As though the letter of communication itself becomes a part of infrastructure—like how the Bible, through constant interaction with its contents, becomes not merely a document, but an exemplification of infrastructure.

REEXAMINING CLASS SYSTEMS

CLASS SYSTEMS are noted for their ambivalent disagreement with realistic social bonds and specifically in their alienation of human stature and possibly even rights. Since this broaches political concern, psychological health, and sociality, dismantling class systems seems to be the obvious choice for avoiding these complex and important aspects of a functioning society and individuality.

First, we must note that, in terms of a political perspective, there is no real matter of individuality except in how the state postures individuality according to their constitution. Genuine individuality is not state-bound but is an entirely different inquiry, in this case, psychological health.

In the arena of mental balance and avoidance of psychological dysfunction, it seems that human stature is an important component. Dismantling stature seems to correlate with improved psychological health. This would be under the jurisdiction of the health department in any given political spectrum, meaning it remains an aspect of the political umbrella.

If we approach the notion of psychological health in the individual context, then human stature—or one's relationship to sociality—is not a concern. Sociality is a construct of society, not of an individual, and goodness or correctness in one society is not the same in another.

In discussing the acquisition of genuine individuality, psychological health is best understood as a function of developmental progression—specifically, whether one has advanced meaningfully from their ancestral psychological starting points. In this view, the primary concern lies not with societal norms or structures, but with the individual's internal development.

This perspective recalls the foundational concerns of early psychological theorists, who were largely preoccupied with the complexity of mental life. While aspects such as physical stature were sometimes considered, they were often set aside due to their political and social implications. Instead, early psychologists focused primarily on sexuality, sexual development, and familial structures, regarding these as the most viable frameworks through which to understand psychological complexity.

Returning to the subject of class systems, it seems to be a concern for the political biosphere alone. The psychology inherent in class systems, in which it does not intersect with those affairs, would not be affected by it. Therefore, we must conclude at this moment that the concerns of class systems— whether positive or negative—are societal concerns, not individual ones.

Yet, if we are to prove that class systems benefit individuality independent of the political biosphere, then we must approach the subject wholeheartedly, considering the individual who has not yet entered the already claimed sphere of political concern.

As we have noted in other works, anything politically oriented will merely overlay the already formatted infrastructure and could only add or subtract, but barely become intrinsic to it. The dystopian society governed by politics is the political umbrella so thorough intact that no genuine social infrastructure is left, and with that characteristic it becomes its own degeneration. Whatever infrastructure remains—because there will always be some—will have free thought or action so permeable that it becomes the real and genuine state. This will be the only justification for continuing control, as they require genuine infrastructure to enable their vitality, creating a contaminated symbiotic relationship that is the narrative of any portrayal of such societies.

Class systems will be an important subject for individual health in more determinate language; individuality devoid of political concern. What class systems do is provide an ample identity to separate and regulate social systems. If we take a grouping of social beings and place them together but attempt to remove the plethora of class integration, we are left with just a random array of individuality. Consequently, there is no communication between individualities other than individuality itself, forcing each person to approach the other for whatever relevant information is imbued, not by their stature, but by their psychological particles.

This seems like the greater form of sociality, where the dynamic is coerced into a more profound framework of reference. Each individual is referenced from their application of such psychological development. What arrives as the alternative is that there is no reference point other than bare selfhood. Each individual becomes a psychological burden or revelation, only to mirror and expand the other as if such expansion will indulge the dynamic in a more elaborate experience of sociality.

Instead, one becomes more individualistic, since such dynamics do not have a single thread of political reference, and it places the individual on leave from genuine society. Society, by its default nature, is something in attendance to political reference, and in this case, the entire experience is to determine a social experience without that attachment.

Is this not simply another way of approaching the question of class? The issue at hand is not one of material starvation or a general collapse of economic surplus, but rather a conceptual dislocation. It frames class divisions in a way that grants the spectrum a kind of validity, yet without a concrete foundation—especially considering that the contemporary era is, by historical standards, one of unprecedented economic abundance.

Indeed, this touches on a critical point: contemporary economic inequality is less about absolute deprivation—as seen in pre-industrial societies and more about relative disparity. The issue lies not in the lack of material resources for survival, but in the perception and experience of dissimilarity within an affluent context.

The conventional discussion grants the notion of 'class' a kind of theoretical validity in an era where, objectively, most individuals are more affluent than preceding eras. This is what makes the contemporary inequality discourse different from historical class struggles.

In the past, class conflict was often tied to survival—peasants revolting against feudal lords, workers striking against wages in prevention of starvation. Currently, it's framed around comparative disparities in wealth and power, which is why it sometimes lacks a clear economic anchor. Instead, it leans on ideas like: if it is relative inequality, then there is no retracing to a better society, for there will always be relative notions of anything.

The only way out of such a perspective is to devalue the class framework in lieu of another, so that society interacts at another point. For example, in ancient Greece, a tripartite society, as noted by Plato, was preoccupied with a class system of intellectuality. Wealth, which is usually a spectrum, was not the only matter of dynamic influence. They also had the bravery associated with a soldier, which may be the reason *Homer* was a vital canon to that population, as it enabled the construction of this class system.

When we do not have a single class system, one is meant to interact with the other as though they are fully formed interfaces of all human possibility, which is too much for any sociality to demand. It would cause an unhealthy bond, where validation becomes the most important trait. At least each member of one's sociality validates the other in their humanness. The alternative—approaching the other as a molded image—would have one reflect on all their psychological makeup, as there is no mediator of class.

Without a mediator of *class*, every interaction forces a total psychological reflection of the self onto the other, as if there is no filter, no buffer, and no alternative lens. This could explain the deep anxiety in contemporary social structures, where every encounter carries the weight of a private existential affirmation or negation, rather than a stable, structured relationship within a clearly understood hierarchy or system.

According to Dowds et al. (1977), "we believe, however, that therapists typically attribute behavioral differences to social class rather than to cognitive style. Accordingly, it is from this misattribution that social class stereotypes are formed. These stereotypes are partly valid because social class is related to cognitive style" (p. 917).[8]

---

[8] Dowds, B. N., Fontana, A. F., Russakoff, L. M., and Harris, M. (1977). *Cognitive Mediators between Patients' Social Class and Therapists' Evaluations.* Archives of General Psychiatry.

Although the final premise of their study leaves us without a more comprehensive cognitive system, we must attribute at least to some degree that the class system itself is a therapeutic production. Surely, the inferior class would not be suited, as the low tier of any class system is with one foot in that dynamic sphere and one out. They are merely individuals in a society to which a certain class system seems to exclude them.

In that individuality, the therapist would require a new form of cognitive style—one that is more comprehensive, not lesser—to reflect on the developing human in its full capacity, not in its succession within a society, no less within a class system. Yes, stereotypes about class and instances of miscommunication may indeed be factors, but they often arise from a lack of tools necessary to engage with the full spectrum of human individuality. That would require an approach akin to the foundational stages of psychotherapy, where it was not connected to class systems.

Typically, we find class systems demarcated based on cultural class, commodified according to affluence. These are simply identity spheres where there is an approach of currency related aspects, as well as a cultural reference point. There is no inherent superiority in belonging to the cultural class, as culture itself constitutes a distinct identity. It is merely a perspective upon general consciousness. The other side of the dynamic—the less cultured persona—will simply participate in a more direct manner in the consciousness realm, with the regular cultural class sequentially informing it.

We naively assume that culture is the reference point of reality, but it is simply an intersection as an informative metric onto the real infrastructure, or its substantiated consciousness permeation. Although this seems to be argued by varying intellectuals, is it the production of intellectuals?

If one takes a closer look at the phenomenon, they would notice that the social acceptance of what is deemed cultural is based on individuality that partakes in the assembly of infrastructure that validates at that point of reference. Noticeably, we accept this retroactively and view history through the lens of its infrastructure, more so than its cultural upheaval at the time. It is viewed as the pre-war or post-war era, rather than the cultural influences and interests of that time and place.

Certainly, it neither represents a pre-war era just by the fact that it does not know itself to be pre-war until war occurs. It serves merely as a dramatic reference point that marks extended periods in history, offering a synopsis of a particular cultural experience—an experience that becomes the infrastructure itself. The pre-war era functions as a substantiated cultural framework that refers only to itself; it cannot truly be "pre-war" by its own logic, nor can it be aligned with another cultural reference point, largely because we have neglected to examine it critically.

Part VI – The Social Life of Speech

INFLECTION AND RELATIONSHIPS

RELATIONSHIPS INVARIABLY retain the same interactive substance and are only distinguished by the degree of inflection from the agent to the interactive substance. This means, for instance, that the family dynamic will invariably be the same manner of interaction, but its varying distinction depends on the degree of inflection. A state of maturity would have a higher rate of inflection, whereas an infantile state would have a lower rate.

A high rate of inflection occurs when there is a significant distance between the object of interaction and the agent performing the interaction. In between, there is a distance of multiple levels of intermediary substance, creating a bandwidth of information that covers a wide range of themes. For example, the mature individual interacts with their familial structure according to a degree of distance, where the object of interaction exists within a set of criteria, which is then extracted for use across various areas of thought. Rather than merely the baseline interaction (which we could call the nearness of personhood to the object of interaction), there are multiple genres that provide an elaboration of its themes.

When a certain rivalry is placed on the base-layer of interaction, either in its infantile stage (where the rivalry plays out in its baseline form) or its mature stage (where the rivalry is understood in terms of personality traits, masculine/feminine dynamics, societal status, order of birth, first-born/last-born, etc.), the interaction—though still rooted in the base-layer—becomes more than just about the object itself. The object provides an explanatory experience that transcends the family system.

In this case, resentment is not personal, as it would be when the interaction is purely at the base-layer. Rather, it becomes an imitation of resentment that reflects broader themes and elements of research. This is what we consider a high rate of inflection, where the object and interactor are distanced by multiple themes that allow the interaction to rise above its base-layer state. Notice that we are recognizing it as an inflection, so the base-layer remains as it always was, but the inflection allows the communication to succeed in the realm of maturity and the advancement of the psyche.

A low rate of inflection occurs when the base-layer of the interaction is actualized. It is as if they are mere contending genes of a DNA sequence, tossing the choice in response to environmental and genetic factors. For instance, when siblings rival, it may be because each represents one parent in opposition to the other. This is a genetic response to that reciprocity, and it represents the base-layer that is actualized in perennial rivalries with inconsequential outcomes. At no point is there a possibility for a reversal of that dynamic, where the rivalry switches sides and the representation of the parent is revealed.

This can only happen when there is a degree of inflection—when at least one of the participants is willing to engage with the interaction based on various themes of their choosing. They are more than willing to adopt the opposing view because it holds the information they seek. The base-layer will always be contentious, for how could a sibling, representing the existential state of one parent within the rivalry with another sibling (who represents the other parent), transcend their own side? What elements of interaction allow them to see beyond their own perspective, if only they stood at an inflection level and in a space that does not induce existential dread?

This point is critical: when the base-layer is enacted, the entire psyche is consumed with its objectives, as representing the existential reality, devoid of availability for other perspectives. Reciprocation becomes nearly impossible, as the psyche is not available to perceive the other side, enveloping the entire situation.

The possibility of reciprocity arises only when there is a mode of inflection that provides availability for different themes and components of the psyche to stand upon, avoiding the existential engulfment of the psyche. Certainly, one could denounce the mature pathway as an avoidance of the existential base-layer, for it might reach a state of inflection that reflects the true nature of the situation. However, this is why we refer to it as a state of inflection, for it always bends from and toward the base-layer of interaction.

It could be the case that one removes themselves from this inflection and perceives the interaction in a mature state beyond the existential framework, resulting in familial dynamics becoming mere objects of contemporary interaction with no impact on either existential growth or universal reality. Yet, as long as there is a state of inflection, there will be an existential emphasis that lingers behind the interaction, guiding the movement toward the information being reciprocated.

UPSPEAK AND SOCIAL DYNAMICS

IN ADDITION TO RELATIONAL CONFLICT, gendered patterns of speech offer another important lens through which emotional expression and social interaction can be understood. This is a particular style of speech—characterized by a drawn-out, highly expressive, and melodic quality. This discussion focuses on two features often associated with this style: *vocal fry* and *upspeak*, examining their psychological underpinnings and the forms of social exchange they reveal. Importantly, these speech patterns function more as part of a cultural model of social interaction than as a simple stylistic or tonal evolution. As such, they are heavily regulated by personality types and not class, distinguishing them from traditional dialect variations.

The format is mostly the musicality of speech rather than content restricted or standardized. If we do find a case of content related, it is found as a vocal source to the proposed melody, and can be replaced to any other proposed sound. For one may use such a format in the afternoon, and in the evening with another. There is the melody of the voice (high and low rises), the incantation (almost chanting or singing), the pace (sometimes slower, more dramatic), and the emotional layering (sounding playful, ironic, interested, all at once). We must then understand their objective.

The utility of this speech is for the service of emotionally related aspects and can be seen as a conduit to serve an emotional purpose. By 'emotional speech,' we refer to the broad range that includes the circumstance of sensations that travel alongside thought and psyche happenstance. In this way, speech becomes the utility of emotion, rather than being the culmination of its structure.

Melodic speech can make feelings visible, possibly for a positive outcome, but still relied by emotional concerns, whether for oneself or others. It demonstrates openness, friendliness, excitement, or empathy. Alternatively, it avoids sounding harsh or cold. The drawn-out vowels, the rising tones, the musical tone—give a faster pathway to the underlying content and intentionality of its substance, or will be seen, the proposed intentionality.

The perceived lack of seriousness is part of the objective, for any usage of music-to-speech will be offered as a form of comedy. Because the addition of melody creates the display of a performance, and when performing a dialectic in contrast to regular speech, it generates the proposition that speech, the speaker, and the audience have arrived for a performance, even as such was not ordered. In this way, tragic theater is not comedic based on performance because the social circumstance has sought that very performance, rather than it being unsanctioned. It becomes the silly element in a social forum, for it is fundamentally self-degenerating, since selfhood has been blatantly discarded to make room for this performance.

The musical tone is also for psychological purposes, used to display a certain distance between personhood and speaker—so that it appears as if the musical tone is a third party to which they are attracted. It is also in this way that vocal fry occurs: because it is a question not from them, but as if some observer is asking it—one they are watching, but to which they remain speechless. The way speech musicality acts as a kind of psychological mediator between the speaker and what is being said. It often does seem like one is not participating in the statement, but rather quoting it, floating alongside it, or commenting on it. It's as if: "I'm saying this, but also observing myself saying it, and inviting you to observe this too." This protects the speaker emotionally: if the statement is wrong, awkward, or vulnerable, it's not entirely the self—it's one riding along with a tone.

The creaky, low energy—often at the end of sentences—suggests detachment. Vocal fry often implies: "I'm not emotionally invested in what I just said; I'm just reporting it like an outside observer." Its speech that can resemble a kind of commentary on the act of speaking: "This isn't really me speaking from my core; I'm presenting a stylized version of speech." This creates ambiguity—a deliberate space between speaker and content.

PSYCHOLOGICAL PURPOSE: EMOTIONAL RISK MANAGEMENT

Instead of standing fully behind every word, the musical tone says: "Here's something I'm fluctuating about... and I'm friendly with it... but I'm not rigidly tied to it." The musical tone creates a third entity in the dynamic: Speaker, Words, and *Performance Atmosphere*. The listener can—and arguably must—play among them. For what can be the response? They are saying nothing of genuine substance, for in their response, there already is an acceptance and regulation that this performance is dynamically interactive.

More so, it is interactive despite its construction. Any form of engagement would result in a loss, for nothing can secure their position. If interactive as if it were personal, it would leave them vulnerable amidst an environment that has not shared that exposure. And if they were to continue the performance, they would, in part, be devoid of individuality.

Almost as if the engagement from the outset is a criterion to destabilize individuality—and the mere validation of engagement becomes a basis for resentment. Ironically, this very format is generated to protect and stimulate heightened emotional realms.

The emotion, if protective, isn't so much to facilitate a generality that doesn't prescribe personhood in the scenario, but more so to anchor the conversation away from individuality. It makes the interaction seem as though there's a world forum awaiting communication, to which the speaker is merely in attendance.

We could see this speech in most sitcoms, where it almost feels like no one is speaking, but rather repeating lines from the surface. It's not so much about protecting the emotion of experience, but rather removing individuality from the scenario—thus preventing individuation and interaction.

This would constitute a display of the representation of context. In short, there is an emotion of protection, and we can see the difference in intention between emotional protection and third-party anchoring. When it is the former, we find that individuals will pronounce the musical tone with dramatic expressiveness—so *upspoken*, so over the top—that it appears as if the emotional realm is being contained. The speech is amplified by its subconscious rejection of the occurrence.

The musical tone is then offered as if it's a third-party announcement, speaking upon us about the troublesome nature of their emotional experience. This tone both protects them and provides ample mechanisms to propose reprisal upon the other party.

In some sense, the environment itself is speaking this tone—this idea, so that it must be true because it is not me speaking it, but rather the occurrences of our surroundings. It is not even available for contemplation—it is simply the fact of existence. Thus, it not only drives the contender to the passé of unavailability for interaction or opinion, for it is beyond the pain—it is already a simple fact of reality, a third-party observer of unabridged scenes and occurrences.

The other case of usage or utilization—to anchor it—is simply the removal of individuation, so that the conversation can progress in a manner that doesn't revolve around the nuances of individualities. This allows the circumstances of content to be more broadly reached, without restraints.

EMOTION OF PROTECTION VS. ANCHORING AWAY FROM INDIVIDUALITY

Emotional Protection - In this case, the musical tone protects the self. It softens vulnerability and signals emotional exposure while simultaneously guarding against that very exposure. The speaker still feels individualistic—they are just shielding themselves. It is reactive: "I feel something and I must shield my core sentiment through this outward musicality."

It's the voice crying through the guise: "Look at me... but please don't hurt me." The musicality becomes weaponized: both a defense against emotional individuation and a passive way of inflicting criticism or distancing the other party. Protection included with a possibility of passive retaliation, all the while, still remaining animated, emotional, tense, and protective.

Third-Party Anchoring (Non-Individuation) - In this case, the musical tone is not about emotional protection. It's about removing personhood from speech altogether. The speaker detaches from platforming individuality as the presentational frame of what's said. Speech becomes surface-level—almost like the characters of a sitcom reciting a script written by an unseen hand. The speaker disappears into the flow of social atmosphere.

There is no existential investment, no real dynamic of dialogue happening between individuals, because they are both platforming away from a genuine persona. So even if there were an exchange, it wouldn't carry a reputable concern for true personhood. Instead, speech becomes a performance—a shared world of floating scripts, an abstract forum.

The musicality here is not about protecting vulnerable emotions; it's about preventing individuation altogether— keeping conversation depersonalized, generalized, and context-driven. Thus, this creates: disappearance into social context, no ownership of ideas or emotions and speech becomes like an ambient environment rather than a personal exchange.

PERFORMING EMOTION

When emotional protection dominates, we arrive at personal drama culture—overreaction, sensitivity, emotional theater. Although it is usual to accuse one party of overreacting, it is rather the entirety of the communicative form that is responsible, including both the parties in the dynamic and any observers.

When third-party anchoring dominates, we get depersonalized mass speech—where no solitary individual truly speaks, but communication is pre-scripted. Not in the sense of a prepared dialogue, but in a de-individualized form that reflects a reduced version of personhood shaped by environmental elements.

Both trends weaken individuation—either by restricting the self in responsive armor or by dissolving the self into ambient social templates. In both cases, true individuality, true dialogue, and true relation between two sovereign persons become harder. Conversation becomes either: an emotional performance, or a social ritual.

TRAGEDY VS. COMEDY

Tragic Speech (Emotional Protection) - In tragedy, characters speak from the depths of their purported version of themselves. Their words arise from emotional pain, are confined by responsibility, and thus open to guilt. These are life-or-death expressions.

When contemporary speech slips into dramatic upspeak and emotional protection, it secretly mimics a tragic pattern: *"I'm putting emotion into this—just look and see."* In essence, speakers dramatize emotion by framing it as a last stand, a final breath of courage within a tragic circumstance.

There is shielding through musicality—just as tragedy in theatre is buffered by its lyrical performance. One cannot survive full tragic exposure. Thus, contemporary musical tone is a muted tragedy. It seeks to express raw emotional reality—though this is fundamentally impossible due to the distance between language and sensation—and instead, communicates the consequences of revealing true vulnerability.

This is not born of fear, but of effective communication that avoids breaching the emotional reserves of sentient beings. Instead of saying: *"I love you!"* (Raw, tragic, existential speech), the contemporary tone says: *"Sooo... like... I just think you're, like... amazing...?"* This is tragedy seen through a veil.

The objective, at least initially, was to create a platform of communication that could be broadly accessible once individuality was removed. Take, for instance, the scripts of most sitcoms. These are only generalizable because of this depersonalization. In a sense, it's the admiration of the comedic genre in its most fundamental form—devoid of individual mortality. But rather than rely on a comedic arc, it places the subject of comedy in the form of speech itself—even more than in the content of that speech.

Comic Speech (Third-Party Anchoring) - In comedy, characters exist in a world of surfaces. They are playful and remain ambitious despite existential circumstances. They play the roles—in both senses of the word. Contemporary third-party anchored speech reflects this comic mode. It differs by appearing in everyday speech and discourse, but is notably absent in more melancholic, bureaucratic, political, or generational contexts. The speaker might say: *"Literally, everyone thinks that."*

The word 'everyone' is ambiguous; the act of thinking and judging is often untrue or irrelevant. The statement holds no real bearing except for the emotional burden it conveys. Thus, contemporary speech laden with musicality is the voice of depersonalized comedy: constant movement, no real suffering, no true consequences.

Sitcom dialogue mimics third-party anchored musicality. It creates a world-forum of easily processed, unthreatening emotions. Speech becomes display, not encounter. Thus, it would feel like commentary rather than lived experience. It feels like a safe, ambient performance. It avoids tragedy by embedding life inside comic form. Everything is relatable and recognizable, but barely existentially dangerous.

CONTRIVED INTIMACY OF A SITCOM

Sitcoms share a single underlying thread. This commonality presents a misconception regarding the material dynamics of individuals, friendships, and intimacy in an adulated form.

This thread suggests that on-screen friendships are expressions of the true nature of friendship itself—depicting the complexities of navigating contemporary society—yet without the actual consequences of existing within that very civilization.

Contemporary entertainment frequently highlights contradictions in romantic dynamics, offering insight into unspoken conceptual tensions. Consider, for example, the phrase: "He treats me like a queen—except at night when he treats me like the naughty girl that I am." While such lines are often delivered in humor, their deeper resonance lies in an unresolved conceptual dissonance between societal roles and intimate identities. The dichotomy between 'queen' (respect) and 'naughty' (disregard) is a deeply indicted issue. One cannot impose this ideation upon friends without shifting the discussion into a more abstract, representational forum— where it becomes a subject of analysis rather than an interactive dynamic.

This kind of expression belongs to the private sphere, even without expression beyond the mind. If one were to introduce it into a friendship, the response would not be on a personal level but rather a representational one. Friends, in their own engagements with societal norms, would not process such a statement in an interactive way; instead, they would approach it as a conceptual study of that very dichotomy. Engaging with such an expression would require acknowledging its complexity and offering a dynamic inference—one that is as conceptual as it is philosophical.

A character grappling with a sexual dichotomy inhabits a worldview where two realms coexist: the *interactive* realm of proportionality and domestication (*being treated like a queen*), and the *representational* realm of disregard (*being treated in a dismissive manner*). The latter can only be understood as a representational element because, fundamentally, we would certainly not accept a worldview that endorses disregard without an overarching system of engagement, where the experience of disregard remains purely experiential and not intrinsic.

Therefore, when a friend enters this arena, they do not resolve the complexity; rather, they amplify it. Yet, there remains a longing for friendships to fulfill such roles. In reality, this dynamic cannot manifest within personal relationships, but sitcoms allow it to exist as a possibility. They sidestep the civilization from which they emerge, creating a realm where such interactions can unfold without the real-world consequences that would otherwise render them untenable.

This same contrivance is evident in scripted dialogue, where personal and deeply intimate exchanges are delivered with an almost rehearsed precision. Consider, for instance, a character's pep talk to loved ones in an extraordinary circumstance. The way the scene is constructed exemplifies the sanitized, choreographed nature of television friendships. The monologue is delivered in a precise rhythm, as the speaker introduces themselves and defines their role in a way that is both efficient and effortlessly humorous: *"Hello, dear ones. I'm here for you through every twist and turn of this journey."*

This is a meticulously crafted line, designed to merge humor and character insight in a way that is instantly digestible.

This is why we find a peculiar fixation upon these fictional friendships: in a highly conscious environment where everything is laden with representational elements, certain interactions cannot be communicated from a personal standpoint but only in furthering the surrounding narrative and context. There is a very good reason that such idealized friendship groups are an anomaly. Once we enter the sphere of this representation-laden world, we are unable to secure the personal realm in dealing with existential reality.

Surely friendships are possible, but either as mere icons within a representational realm—contextual inferences such as those found in workplace or school settings—or as a means of fulfilling an ideation that furthers one's consciousness framework, such as fame, affluence, or other status emblems. However, there is no room for the authentic notion of friendship since representational elements invariably intrude, preventing interactive exchange.

Maintaining a personal relationship while avoiding topics tied to representational elements presents considerable challenges, leading individuals to conform to surrounding representational norms. Moreover, the resurgence of nostalgia for scripted friendships and efforts to replicate such group dynamics in reality tend to intensify relational difficulties by merging genuine interpersonal exchange with representational frameworks, resulting in unstable dynamics.

RELATABILITY AND SOCIAL INTEGRATION

Sociality, or relatability, is the transference between an interactive sediment and its reintegration within a sequence of consciousness. Without sociality, the integration will be primarily detailed as a product that becomes included within the psyche's apparatus, without so much as participating in the continuum of consciousness.

If we must inquire as to what locale in the psyche could be the habitat of functional thought patterns without their association with consciousness, we find it to be a decommissioned part that serves to map out those details, without relatability to the rest of the psyche. It stands as a unique substructure that relies on a constitution generating a very calculated encapsulation of consciousness—enough to generate stimulation so that the brain can function in an abstract manner, but short of participating in the regular sequence of the psyche.

The further this procedure goes, the more fragmented the parts of the psyche become, and possibly reintegration and relatability are lost. The sociality of the specific interactive element allows that admixture to become integrated because of the application to which the psyche finds in something sociable—but more accurately, animated. When something is animated, it becomes recognized as relatable, and for the psyche, relatability is its most sought-after trait, for then it can connect to its other parts.

RELATABILITY AND RECIPROCITY OF DESIGN

EVERY SOCIAL CREATION contains the data of relatability given to that object or person. We may overlook how this occurs, yet, nonetheless it exists, for which every person can be defined to the degree of social relatability procured towards them, and this is measured in both quality and quantity. Relatability as an impression will only be applicable in the event where there is a communication of sorts between that which has such recognition for its subject.

If, for instance, such relatability is seen from a distance, although in theory an available impression is to be made, the subject does not become accepted into that communion. Even if, in private affairs, one or many have secured enough relatability to be given a great deal to a particular subject, the fact that it hasn't reached the position where a social dynamic is in place makes the development futile.

The subject themselves, or the object of creation, will need to become available for that impression, which for social beings is only when they endure a pressing dynamic so that their psyche becomes apt to such a succession. Not simply the mechanics of exchange are at work, but in how a psyche becomes indebted to an impression which matters.

As we can find with objects—even with great design, if the object does not mold in a kind for whatever reason, or if its production has separated the design and its relatability from garnering an impression that would succeed down the chain of command to the finality of creation—it will lose such communion. And if such relatability, when followed through other social beings which do not foster to a greater degree, does not continue the message or impression to generate a format upon the individual, the sequence breaks.

Parental figures are most apt for the impression of relatability upon the child because the child is available for the impression, it is direct, and there is a social dynamic: the parents want the child's progress by virtue of their parental attachment, and the child wants their parental imprint because they are believed to be the wholesome state of experience, thereby making them the most influential figures to gain that impression upon the child.

If these measures are found, the impression would be most similar, though it is difficult to find social content of such a degree of relatability to garner such an impression. What would motivate someone to develop a system of relatability towards another, unless there is a familial bond?

When we discuss the quality of relatability, we notice that it requires the wholeness of personhood in giving the impression upon another substrate or person. This amicability of wholeness is most found in the parental figure, by the subconscious recognition that the child is the continuation of their entire being—but is not limited to biological lineage. It is, rather, the ongoing communion of the parent in impressing upon the child their presence—and in the child's eventual separation, the continuation of that communion—that constitutes the very form and fullness of parental identity. But not all impression is equal; in the development of the private affairs of the parents—even if they wanted to—by limited scope, the impression will be equally limited.

We cannot have a case where the impression of relatability is greater than the degree of development within the individual giving that impression. Since relatability is in how one reflects onto their correlation modality, what correlates to a greater reflection would garner a significant form upon whatever they choose to be their impression. This is when we question this notion in the case of submission to design, which is the constant innovation of a person onto a particular set of principles to grant them a perfected impression upon substrate or individual.

This seems the way out of this criteria, where despite the relatability that reaches back to the developmental state of the designer, they have set in stone an objective rule that circumvents their relatability so that mass production or codifiers at the reception of those design principles will be able to receive the codex of relatability without recognition or contribution to that very relatability. Two points of departure occur in this process: for one, even if we could somehow imprint relatability into a codex of principles called design, the very next person who takes the design—without the underlying acquisition of that relatability—will not pass it on intact, carrying only the core principles themselves.

The second point of conjecture—or rather degeneration—of the relatability is the connection between design principles and the individual's relatability context, as they are not the same. Relatability is the varying procurement of one's vitality of personhood mirrored in reciprocal dynamics. Without reciprocity, the art piece sits isolated, waiting for the next impartial reception. It faces the artist, who must deal with the impression as their human interface, thus doing surgery on themselves in the continuance of the painting. Even as it is an object, by the constant communion, the substrate takes upon itself the reciprocity of that relatability. This reaches a point where the artist and art piece are felt as a union.

Principles of design, in their theoretical phase, follow a similar process because they are fundamentally a form of artistic endeavor; however, they eventually deviate their course to make way for principles of production rather than the impressions themselves. Once divorced from the design phase and moved to production, there is no symbiotic relationship between substrate and relatability, having followed a new criteria set in the form of production principles.

Moreover, in the design phase, by not including the entire scope of the substrate in its creation, it is removed from interacting with the substrate itself, becoming an artistic endeavor—isolated from the canvas's constant reciprocal motion.

Even when design mimics production with the final substrate, designers do not view the substrate in its full capacity but rather as a single format meant to be mimicked. Thus, the multitude at the final capacity is excluded from reciprocity, leaving only an individualized form expected to be replicated.

One cannot conjure what the process of design would look like if there were a constant stream of relatability between designer and the multitudes of the substrate; there can be no relatability upon more than an individualized substrate, for reciprocity itself limits extension. It is akin to an artist painting the same painting on three canvases; at some point, each will deviate based on the reciprocity between artist and canvas during each impression.

Despite the ostensible awareness that there is a separation—and possibly a complete divide—between design and production substrate, and the design itself only able to procure a single substrate (though recognizing its multitude for replication), reciprocity remains based on an individualized experience between designer and object of design.

There is another limitation: the recognition of what the eventual substrate is for the purpose of design. In regular artistic endeavor, the substrate is clear—the canvas is for the painting, the musical ensemble for the piece of music. In this case, the substrate is not clear: design aims to create a form to be replicated rather than an end in itself. At no point in the design phase can one separate according to production development, nor can one fully include the finality of production in its replicated state; designers are not designing to a specific substrate but to an idea of a substrate, shaped by both production and the idea of replication.

Thus, what is required is a singularity in the substrate or social being for reciprocity between individual and impression of relatability; without it, there is no completeness of personhood, as no dynamic fully falls into place.

Besides the aspect of quality noted for reciprocity, another aspect is the degree of separation between each form of communion. If the impression is attempted as a direct communion of a single stream of consciousness, it will not be considered relatability, because there's no inflection or reflection during the process—it does not relate back to the person but rather secures an idea of what would one think relatability might be, rather than being relatability itself.

DUALITY OF RELATABILITY

RELATABILITY can be conveyed in two ways: as an impressionable aspect of the object or being, or as the object or being becoming intertwined with the mechanism of impression. When there is alignment in the modality of that impression—including the wholeness of the substrate—one becomes attuned to a format in which a diverse space intermediates the intersections, and the two proponents are distinct but symbiotic.

The other way is to have the object become personified such that the individual presumes their adaptability to a single unit, treating the impression upon the object as a perceptual layer of oneself. One then *impressionizes* themselves upon it, as if it were part of themselves, even though such is a hallucination of an external, genuine form. The impression still occurs—the object remains an external relatability—but under the assumption that it is merely an internal experience, weighted by the personification taking hold of oneself.

Until one recognizes this underlying process, it will be a furthest impression without a sequence granting the object a right of separation from one's domain. If the external object is a social being, they cannot partake in this hallucination, as they must verify such as a receptacle for that impression. Still, the impression takes place but is unrecognized by either party— one assuming it internal, the other unavailable to receive such qualities.

This is what we term *tragedy*, where there is no separation of relatability for the impressionable quality, yet the social being receiving that impression is reconstructed for the process. The other mode—alignment between external object and internal impression—is deemed *comedy*, where both gain the symbiotic resolve of that discourse, though nothing is more impressionable than the tragic form.

Both elements form part of a narrative arc: without tragedy—the personification of the object into one's psyche—one does not engage the learning aspect required to participate deeply with the object. It almost requires personification or objectification before moving to external relatability, for the external aspect is unknown to personhood, at least existentially. Hence the necessity of communion between individual and object, reaching a point where personification occurs—where it is tragic for the individual in embodying their object of interest, unable to escape it, becoming a psyche process. Then, upon recognition of distinction, the relatability factor aligns strongly with the object, having been so intimate that separation was unperceived; only then can one finalize that impression by re-establishing their distinct relatability as an external form.